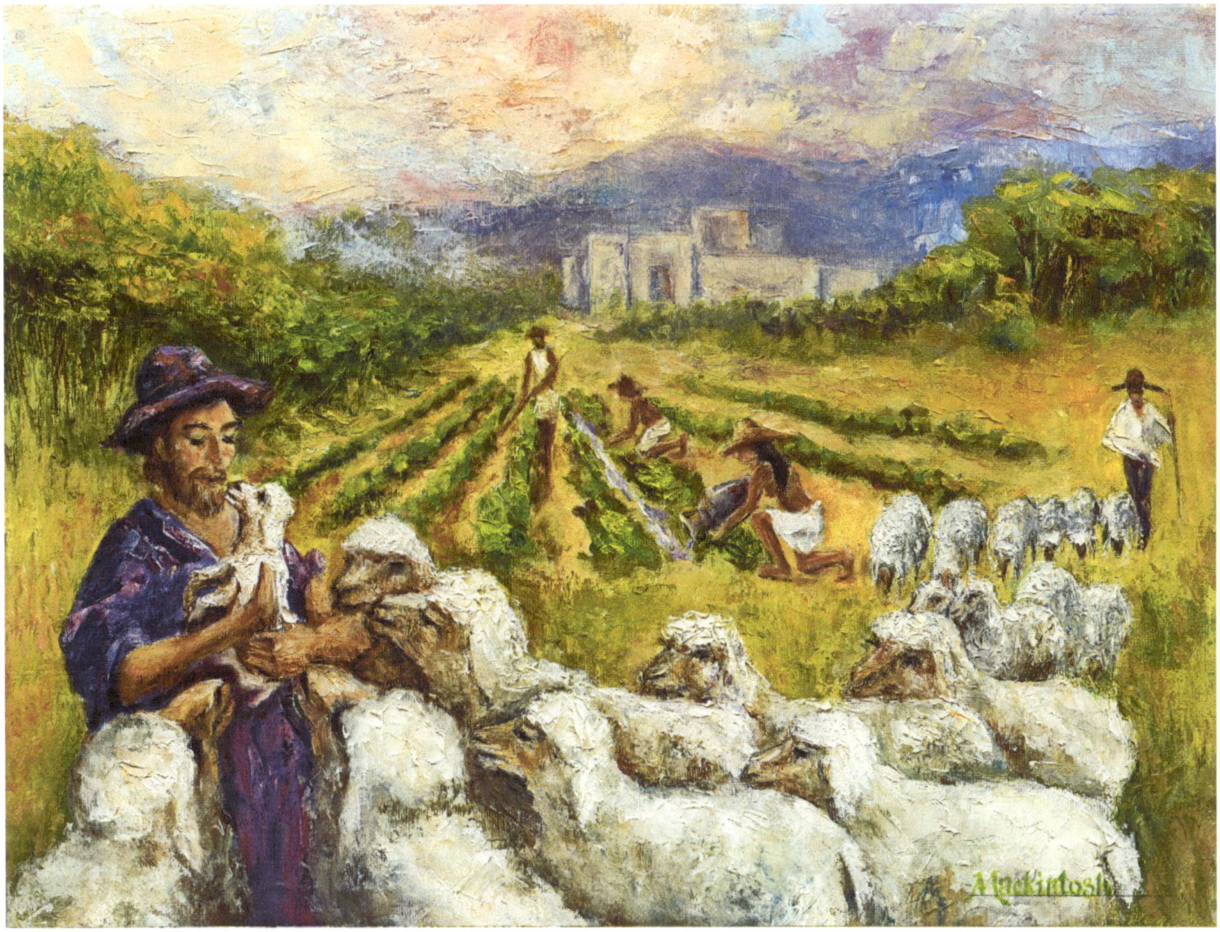

Cain and Abel

A Parable of the Redeemer

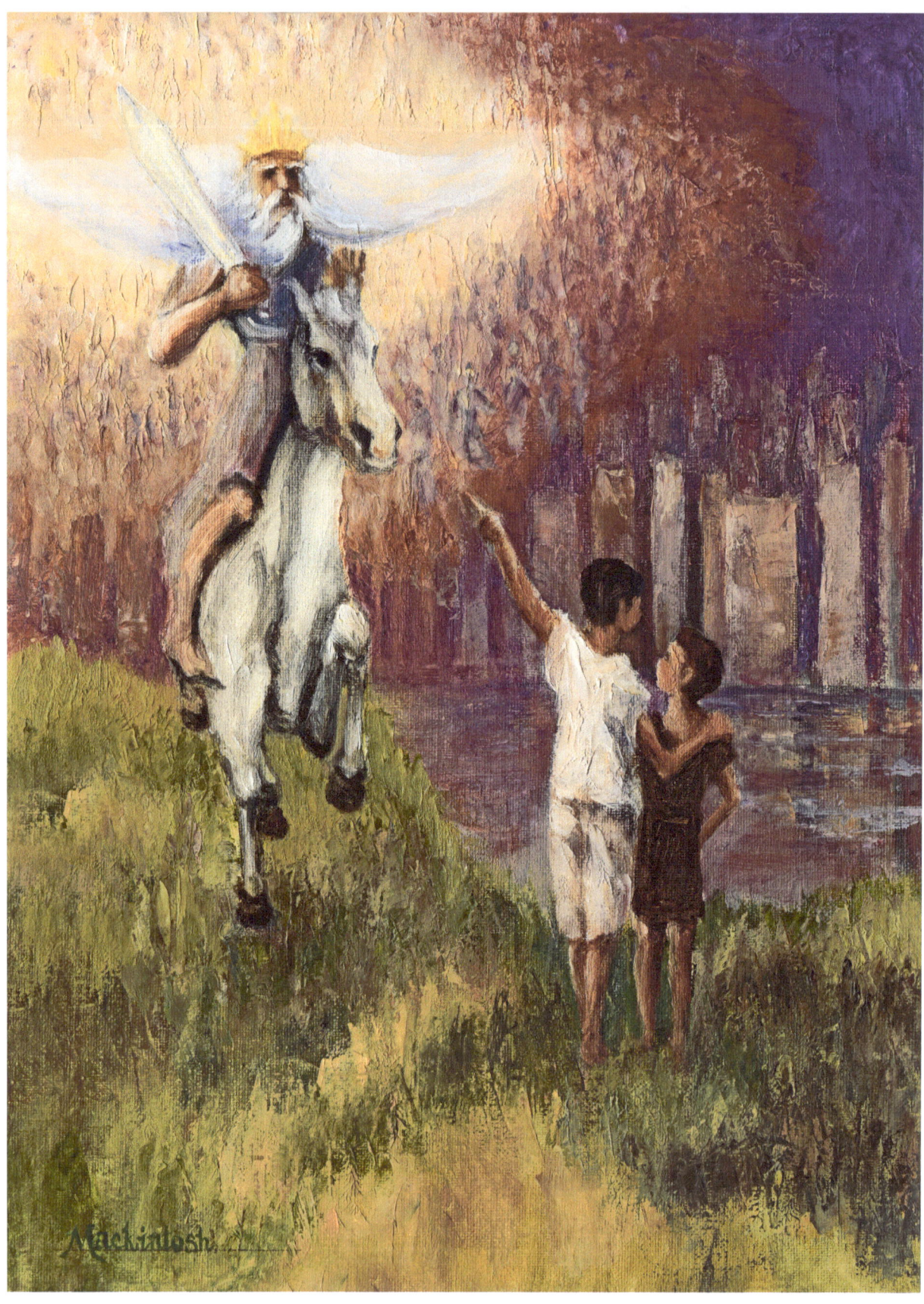

The Prophecy of Enoch

II

A Parable of

The

Redeemer

An Account of Events

Before Adam to before

Noah's Flood

STEVEN MACKINTOSH

Author and Artist

ABOUT THE AUTHOR

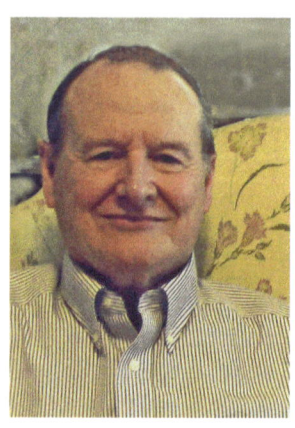

Steven Mackintosh was born in Santa Ana, California on a small cattle ranch where he observed structures, buildings, forms and shapes of animals and people as they worked. His eye was captivated by sunlight playing against shadows. He was determined to capture all that beauty by drawing and painting. At the age of twelve, his mother noticed his inclination and gave him an oil painting set for Christmas.

Throughout his life art and ancient history were his main interests. He earned a degree in business, but his desire was painting. Finally, he retired and his passion took over. In time, the idea came to mind of illustrating historical and biblical stories and events. Thus came this, his first illustrated book: A Parable of the Redeemer.

Very special thanks to my dear sister, Nancy Christiansen, and also David Stuck for their patient editing, help and advice with this book. And special thanks to my wonderful wife Consuelo, who was always there with her consolation and patience. Thanks also to my many other friends that helped with suggestions, comments and compliments while putting this project together.

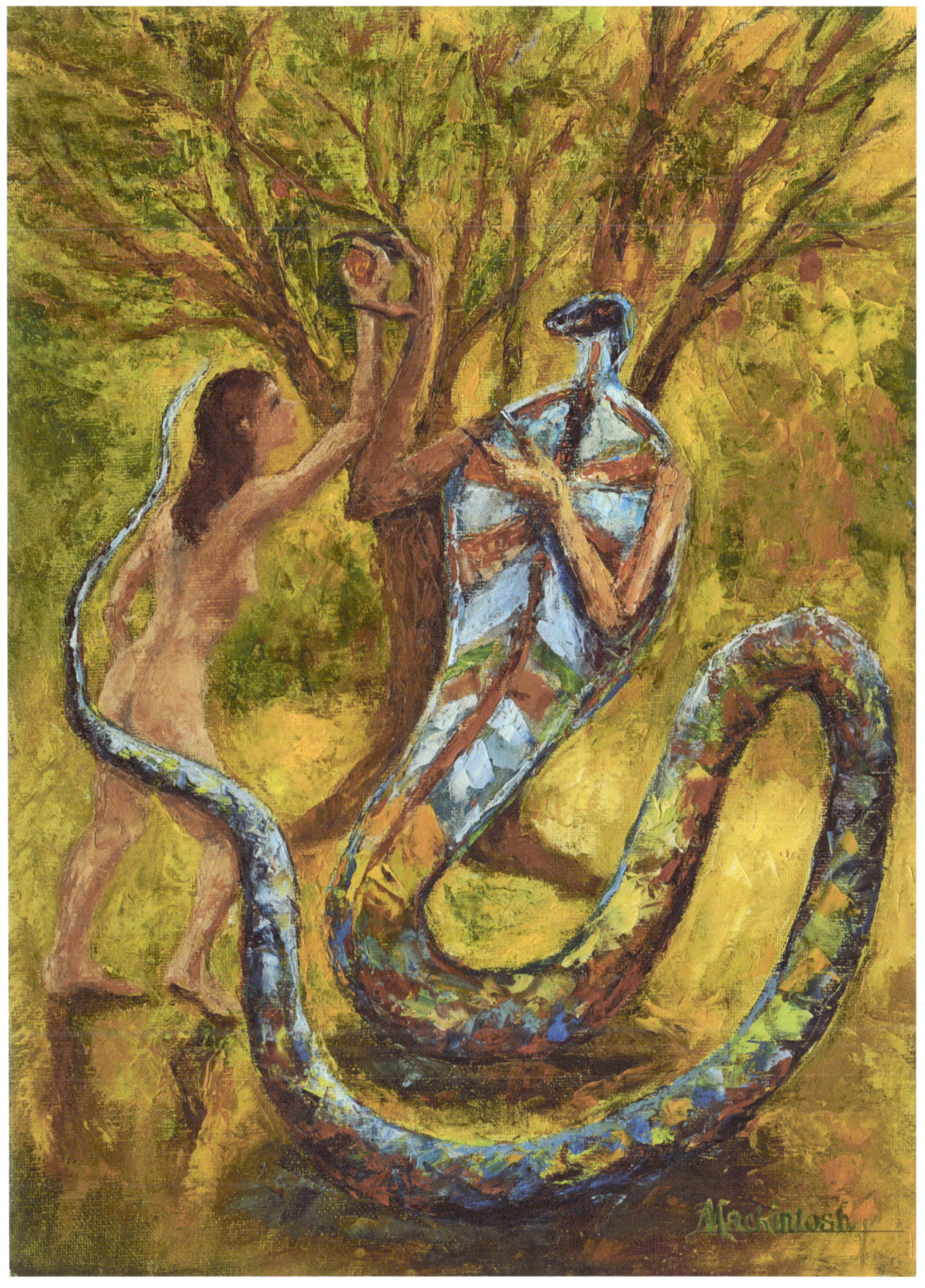

The Temptation and the Fall

V

A Parable of the Redeemer

Contents

A Parable of the Redeemer
An Account of Events before Adam to before Noah's Flood

STEVEN MACKINTOSH
Author and Artist

Introduction

(Psalm 145:17) The LORD is righteous in all His ways and holy in all His works. (Ex 15:11) Who is like unto thee, O LORD, among the gods? Who is like thee, glorious in holiness, fearful in praises, doing wonders? His authority is complete, His wisdom and prudence are supreme and all His judgments are perfect.

Before time and the foundation of the earth our Creator had plans for MANKIND. We were to be the pinnacle of his creation, His special pleasure, created in His own image. His joy would be to have fellowship with us and His delight would be having our love focused on Him, freely given in truth.

Our Creator's law is righteousness and perfect, established by His character, exemplifying the essence of life and light, from which it is impossible for Him to depart. He gave Man the same law to follow by which He Himself abides. His boundaries are not to restrict us but to protect us from the death that sin brings.

When we depart from God's law we drive away His love, joy and peace and invite pain, sorrow, suffering and death into our lives. God calls this sin because it separates us from Him, who is the source of life. The result of sin is death.

This book's illustrations are to portray the series of events from before Adam and Eve's arrival to before the great flood of Noah. Also, to depict how our Creator gave His creation freewill, but how, more often than not, we've turned freewill into self-willed disobedience against Him. Going against His law continues to bring destruction and death to all living on this planet.

More significantly, however, this book's illustrations are to show how, out of His great mercy and gracious love, our Creator reaches out to save mankind again and again from our own self-destruction, making Him not only our Creator but also our Redeemer.

Chapter 1: Before the Beginning

The High and Lofty One that Inhabits Eternity

(Isaiah 57:15) For thus says the high and lofty One that inhabits eternity, whose name is Holy; I dwell in the high and holy place, with him also that is of a contrite and humble spirit....

The Creator created all things for His own pleasure with His perfect laws ruling over all, establishing His holy, righteous character, which cannot tolerate sin. He made man sinless and free so that with Him, we could share the wonders of His creation together.

Freedom is part of the Creator's character. He gave us freewill to love or reject Him, to follow His perfect laws or disobey them, to do His will or our own will. He is wise and knows that love that is coerced, is not true love.

Our Creator is the source of all life and knows the consequence of sin is death. He wants us to live so He gave us His laws to warn us of sin's danger. But mankind soon exercised his own freewill and departed from God's law. This separated man from God bringing upon himself all the ills that afflict today's world including pain, suffering, hatred, death, murder, greed and war.

Not long after this, the human race forgot about the relationship they once had with their Creator. Many began to think that their Creator was too high and distant to bother with the affairs of men. In time, others grew so far from Him that they assumed that He just didn't exist.

Our Creator foresaw our weakness and had a plan to rescue us. Man, by nature, will fall. Our Creator, by nature, is our Redeemer, eager to save us. We may feel that He's too far away to be interested in us, but He is always awaiting our call. His delight is being close to those who have a repentant and a contrite heart. Anyone can be close to Him if they are willing to give up their pride, admit their faults, turn away from sin and ask for His forgiveness. He is our Redeemer.

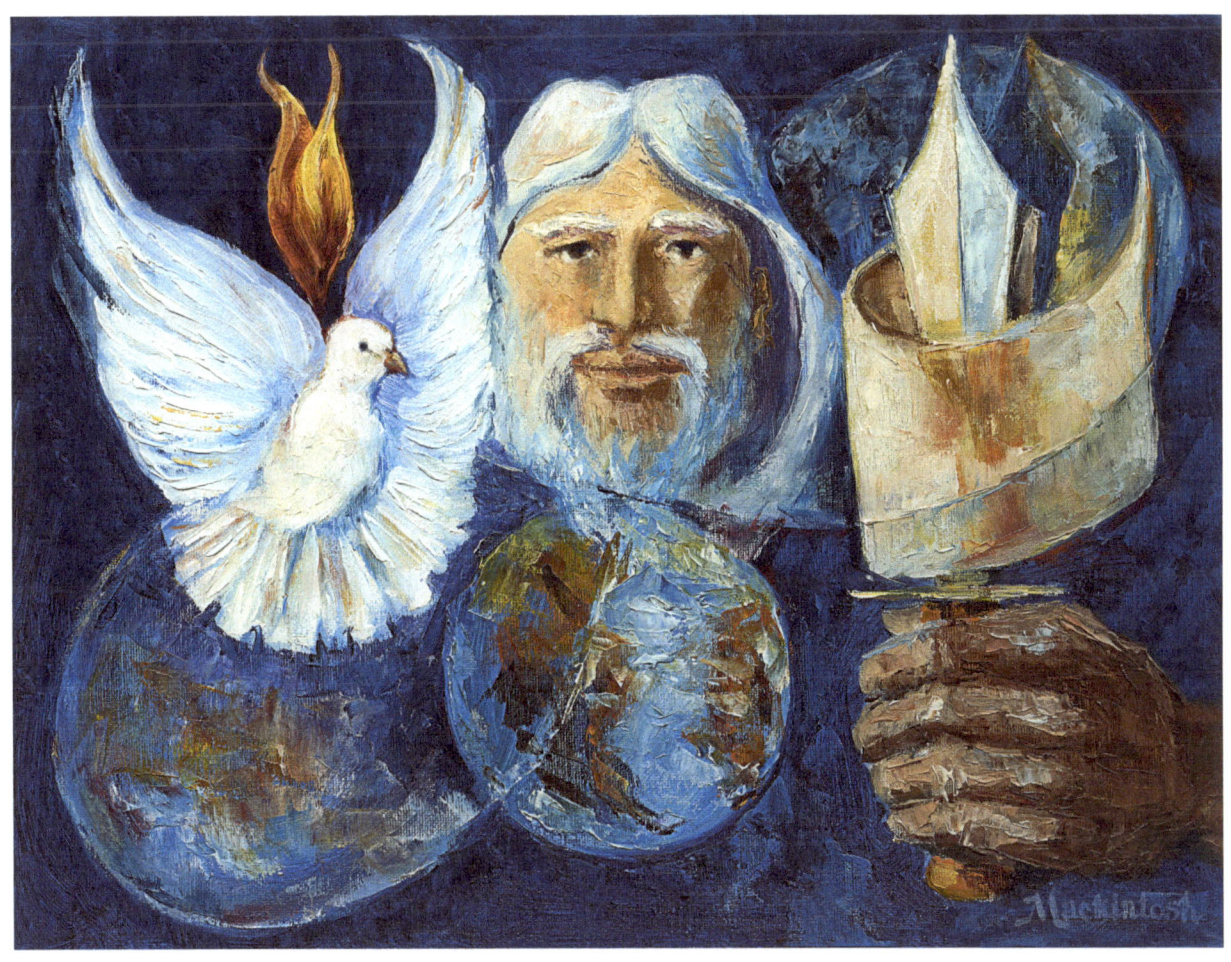

Painting 1: The High and Lofty One

A Parable of the Redeemer

The Discontent

(James 1:13-15) Every man is tempted, when he is drawn away by his own lust, and enticed. Then when lust has conceived, it brings forth sin: and sin, when it is finished, brings forth death.

There was a man that had everything going for him. He had the highest rank and stature over all his fellows. He had castles, palaces, and more riches than anyone, yet he was unhappy. He thought of himself worthy of a greater position even as he advanced to greater and greater heights. His pride eventually took control of his thinking to the point of obsession—he should be the greatest of all. There was a great obstacle standing in his way: the King.

His frustration grew as he endured this complete injustice. Surely his wisdom exceeded that of the king. But the king would always be on top and he always a servant… the servant of a foolish king. That would never change unless he took things into his own hands.

Have you ever known someone that had everything going for them but insisted that they deserved better? Or maybe you've known someone who has it better than you, and you think you deserve better than them. I've been that way. Finally, the Creator taught me the art of thanksgiving. Then discontentment faded and life became fulfilling.

The world today finds itself in the condition where things will never be fair or just. Giving thanks, however, changes our attitude. Then we will see our Creator multiply the blessings He's given us. He is our Redeemer.

The Discovery

(Isaiah 14:12) How art thou fallen from heaven, O Lucifer, son of the morning…! (Ezekiel 28:15) You were perfect in thy ways from the day that you were created, till iniquity was found in thee.

The man described above was Lucifer. He had the highest position of all God's angels. He was the wisest, highest ranking angel: the "Covering Cherub" of the Creator, conducting praise and worship in the courts of heaven. He ruled over one third of the heavenly hosts. The only being in all creation higher than him was his Creator.

One day, to his alarm and frustration, he discovered that the Creator had a plan to create a different kind of being, to be called MAN, to be made in his own image—the very image of the Creator. Along with this, he learned that he was preparing a special environment on the planet Earth where man could live, enjoying all the pleasures of the Creator's abundance.

"Had God lost his mind?" questioned Lucifer. He felt the Creator had just slapped him in the face. "How am I supposed to tolerate such an insult?" he questioned. "This must be avenged," he shouted. Rage against his Maker filled his heart. Egotism shot from his lips as he rehearsed his grievances aloud as envy boiled up from his bones. "After all my service to him, I deserve better than this," he thundered. "Why couldn't He make me in His own image?" he argued. "But no, I'm just an angel." "Well I'm sick of always coming out in second place," he contested. "I'll get back at him somehow. The Creator must pay for treating me with this contempt… as if I were second class."

Envy can enter our heart when others receive what we think we deserve. Pride enters clouding our vision from seeing our Creator's blessings. We demand that justice be done. But if justice were truly done would we then be happy? It may be that if True justice were dealt we would receive harsher punishment. Our Creator is gracious and merciful when dealing out justice. But he comes down hard on pride. Learn to thank Him for His blessings, His kindness and compassion on our weaknesses. He is our Redeemer.

3

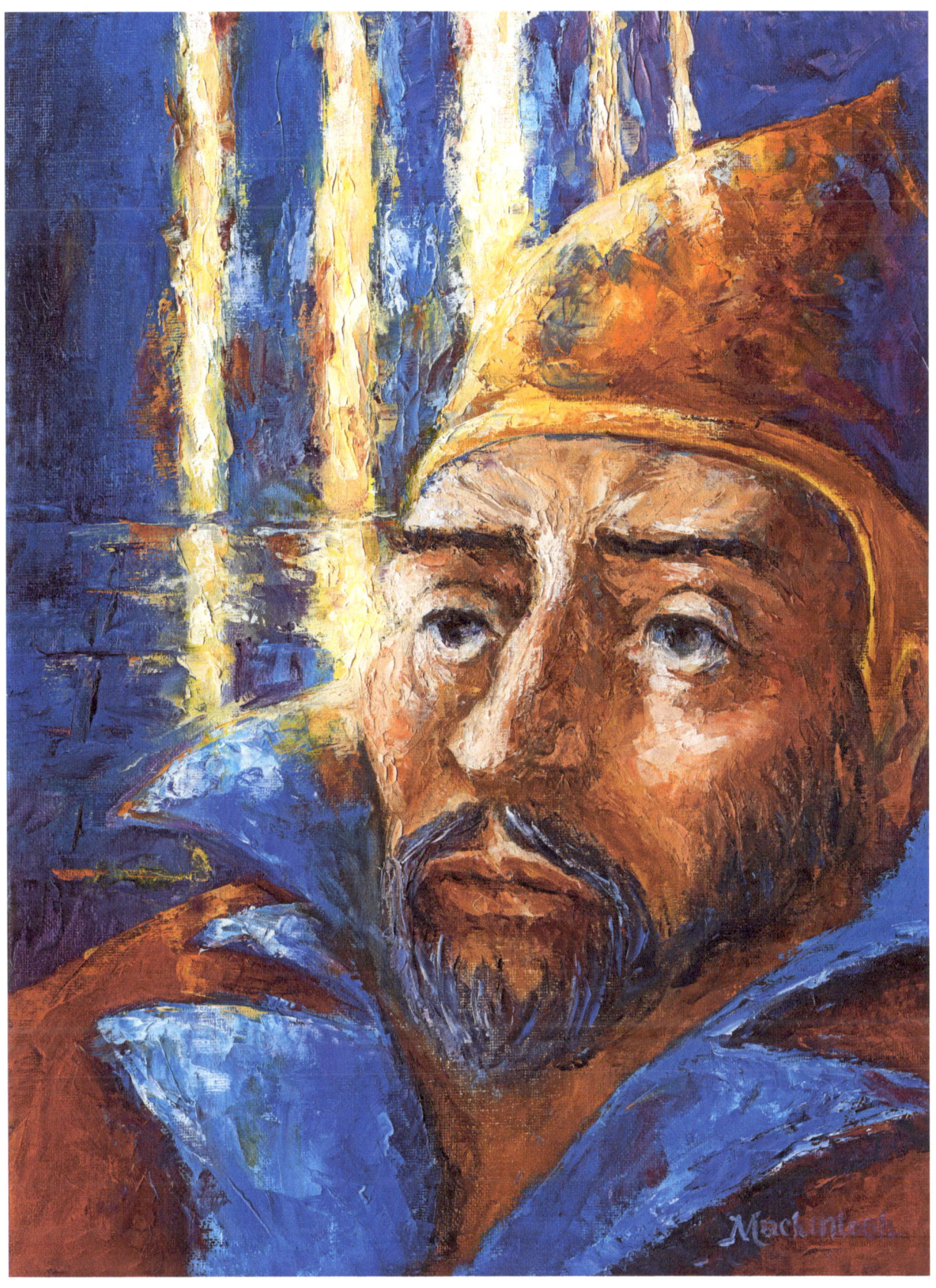

Painting 2: The Discontent

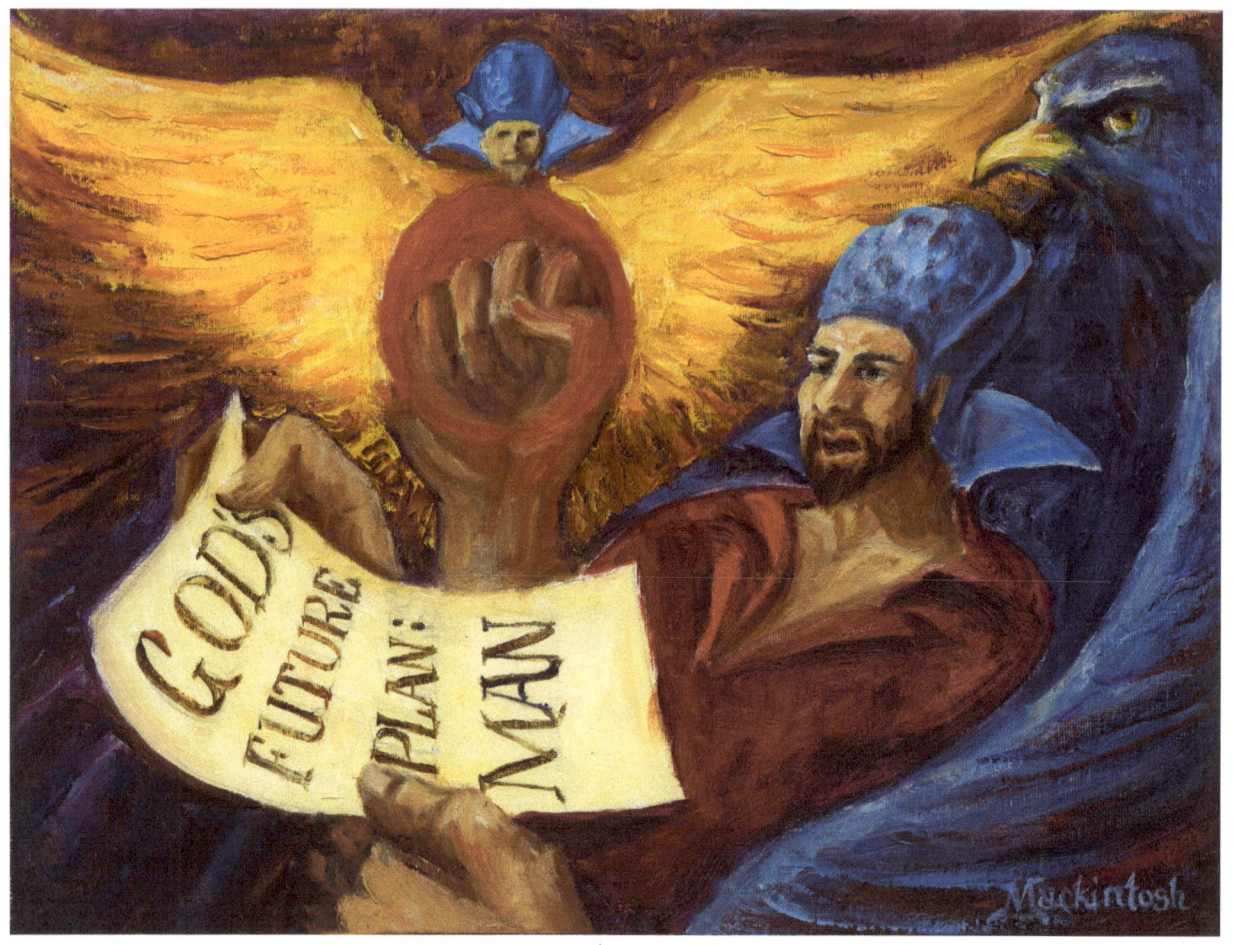

Painting 3: The Discovery

The Rebellion

(Ezekiel 28:2) The Lord GOD says this: because your heart is lifted up, and you have said, I am a God, I sit in the seat of God....because of thy beauty; thou hast corrupted thy wisdom by reason of thy brightness.

Lucifer, imagining himself to be wiser and stronger than his Creator, he decided to take things into his own hands. He planned to overthrow the Creator and assume the highest position for himself. He reasoned that the Creator, who is loving and merciful, was also weak and sorrowful and would offer little or no resistance. God's throne would be his for the taking.

Lucifer mustered all his angels: one-third of all the heavenly hosts and went to war against the Almighty. He hadn't considered that the very character of the Creator cannot tolerate sin. He hates it. Additionally, there's nothing that brings on the wrath of the Almighty faster, with more ferocity, than pride and rebellion. So what Lucifer assayed to be a short skirmish, cost him dearly. And history, after tallying its final assessment, will prove dreadful to him and all who follow him.

Who would dare to take up arms against their Creator? Who would be so foolish? Mankind does it all the time. Our Creator is not shortsighted. He sees every secret plan we make. He knows it before it's acted. He knows every thought before it is considered. We make our plans in secret because we want our will to be done, not His. Are we wiser than our Creator? Since He is full of love and mercy why do we so often abuse his grace? Our society tolerates sin, but that doesn't

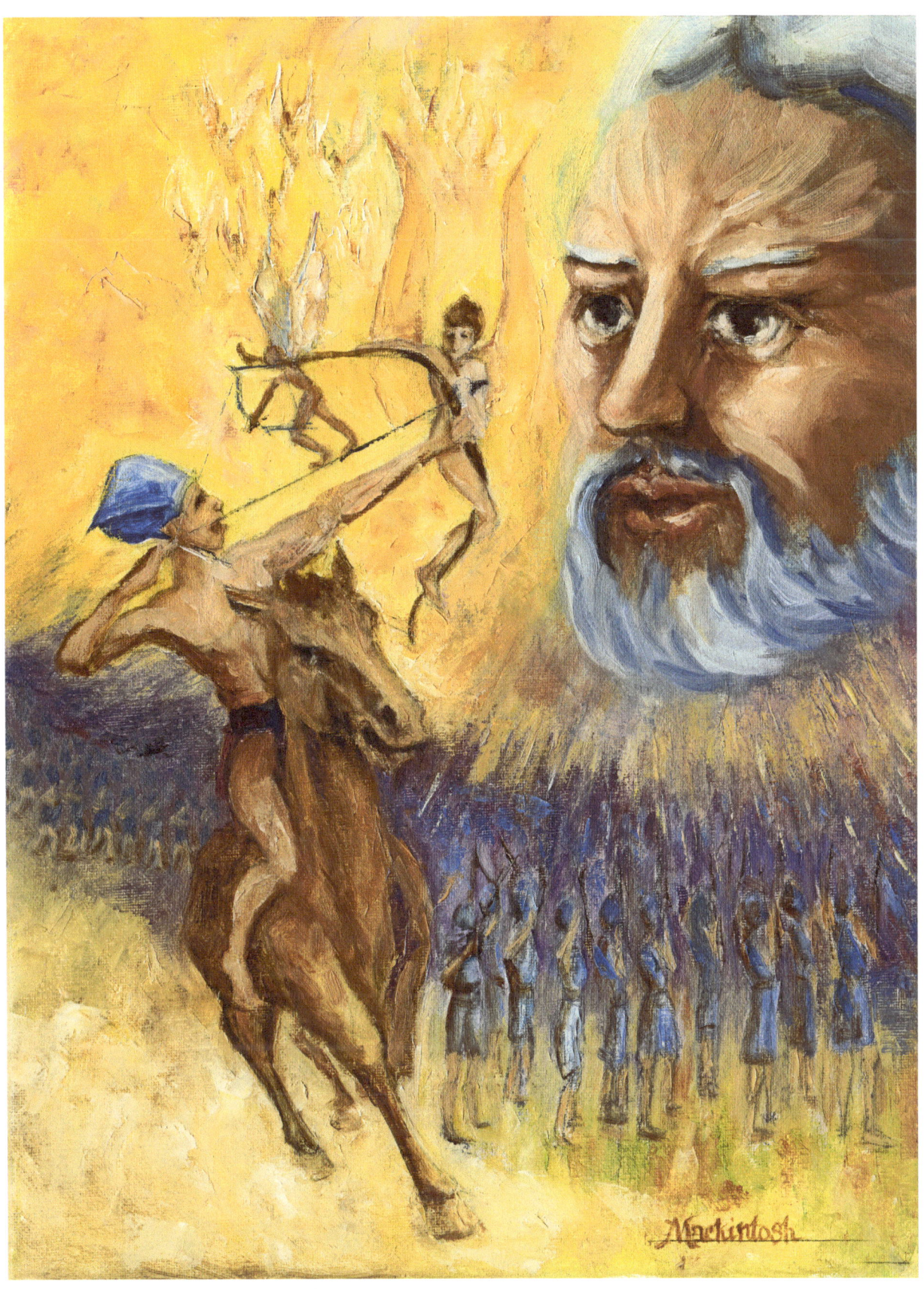

Painting 4: The Rebellion

mean our Creator does. He is the same yesterday, today and forever. He has always hated sin and hates it still. His laws still stand. Being human, we think He will bend to accommodate social pressure: our will over his. Then, after we get our own will, in despair we cry to Him for mercy to save us from the consequences of our error. That is what he's been waiting for. He is always our Redeemer.

How art thou Fallen… O Lucifer…

How are you fallen from heaven, O Lucifer, son of the morning! How are you cut down to the ground….(Isaiah 14:12). Your heart was lifted up because of your beauty; you have corrupted your wisdom by reason of the brightness: (So God said) I will cast you to the ground; I will knock you down in front of kings, that they may plainly see you (Ezekiel 28:17).

As Lucifer fought against his Creator, the foundation where he stood gave way, crumbled and fell from beneath his feet. Without God there is no foundation. There was no Rock of salvation for him.

So the Creator demonstrated to the entire universe that He is Almighty God. There is none above Him. He is holy, righteous and no sin can exist in His presence. By the great Word of His Power the Creator cast Lucifer out of heaven to the ground. Because of his rebellion, pride, greed and envy he was banished from God's holy presence. However, he would continue to have access to the lower regions of the heavens as "prince of the power of the air," and the "prince of darkness," from where he can still shout out accusations against the saints as he did with Job. Lucifer's eviction from heaven's holy sanctuary demonstrated to all, even to the very greatest of the Almighty's angels, that the Creator is Almighty. He has no tolerance for sin and He will execute righteous judgment on all who choose to defy Him.

Because the Creator is just, we can be certain that Lucifer was given every opportunity to repent. But pride and lust for power convinced him that his own lies were true, that being wiser he deserved the Creator's throne. Finally, the Almighty gave him over to believing his own lies, which he was determined to believe. Lucifer is a liar and the father of lies. He will never change. Those who believe their own lies and those who believe Lucifer's lies, both live in falsehood.

Today's reasoning tells us that society owes us a better life, that it's okay to take from others who "have," because being "less fortunate," we deserve better. That reasoning questions our responsibility before our Creator. Those who have much must give an account for much and those who have little must also. We will all stand or fall when judged by our Creator for our faithfulness. Jealousy is being covetous of others. He has given you what you can handle. Put the little that you have in His hands and allowed him to work through you. That takes faith! Let's be thankful and faithful for what has been given us by our Redeemer.

All the hosts of heaven rejoiced at the Creator's victory as the first round of the battle between Lucifer and the Almighty ended with the devil being cast down to the ground—to earth. *And the earth was without form and void; and darkness was upon the face of the deep, (Geneses 1:2).*

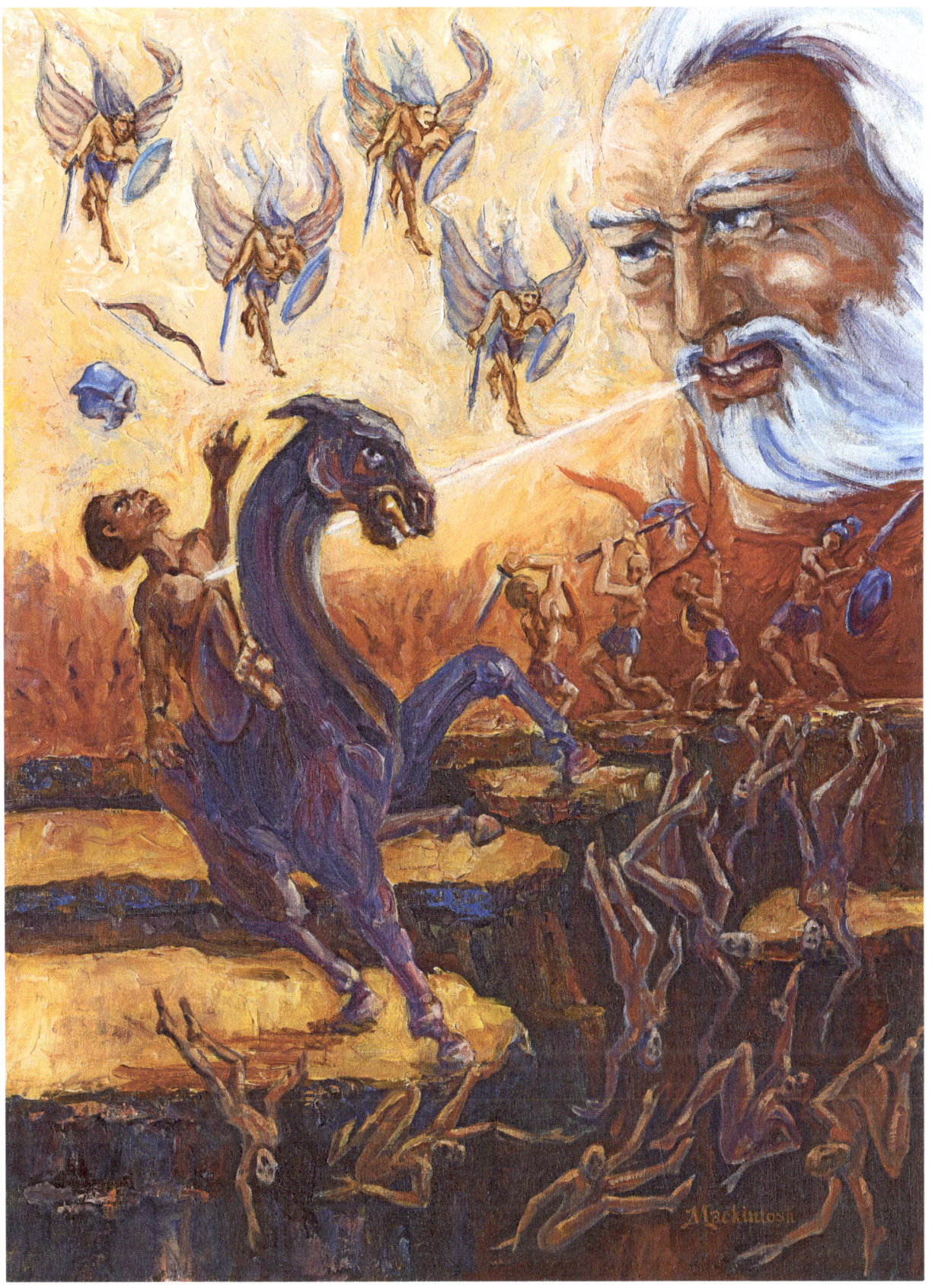

Painting 5: How art thou Fallen… O Lucifer…

Chapter 2: And God Said…

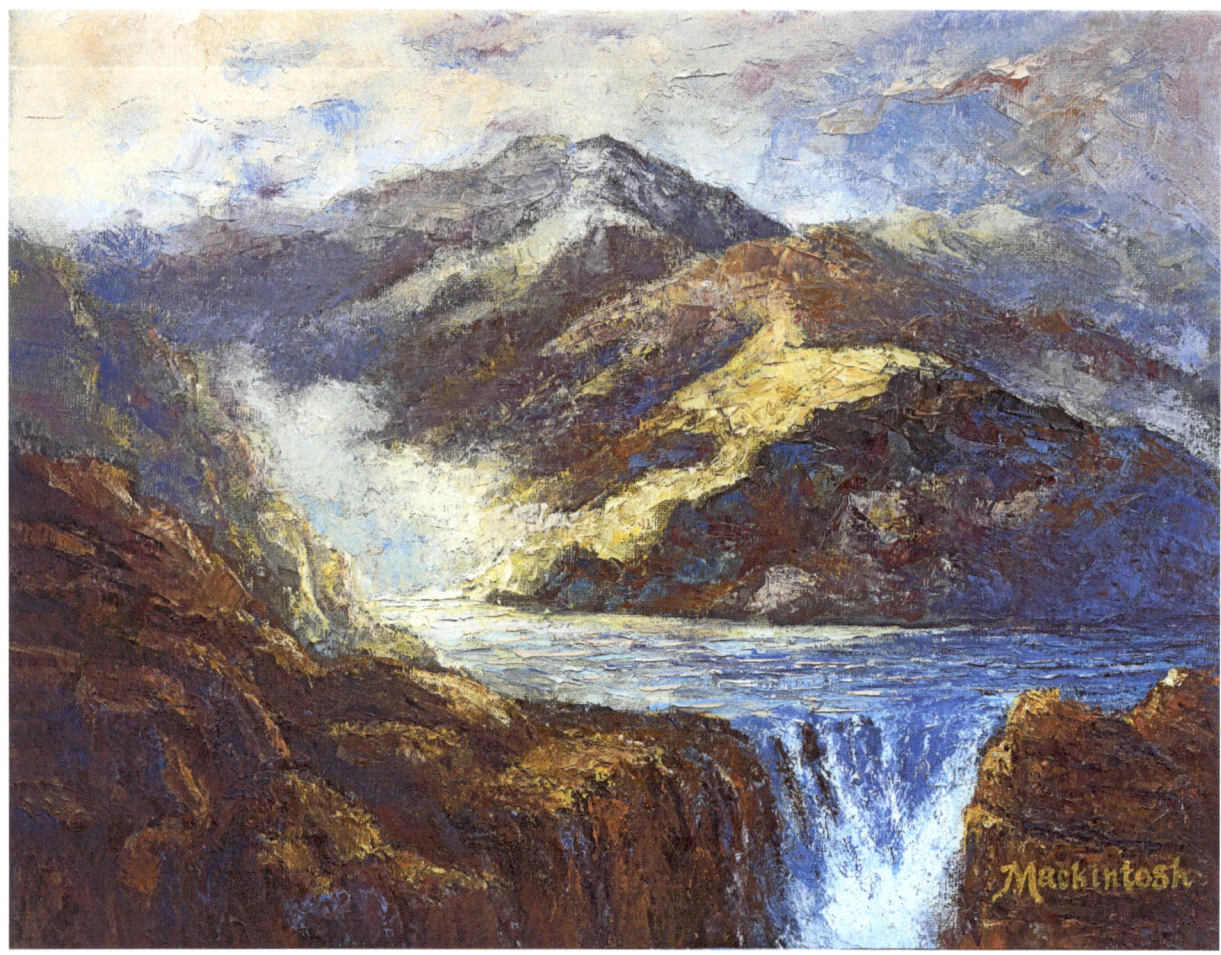

Painting 6: And God said, "Let there be light."

(Hebrews 11:3) Through faith we understand that the worlds were framed by the word of God, so that things which are seen were not made of things which do appear. Psalms 33:6, By the Word of the LORD were the heavens made; and all the host of them by the breath of His mouth.

The Creator reveals Himself through His works. (Psalms 19:1), *The heavens declare the glory of God; and the firmament shows His handiwork."* The things that we see (God's creation) were not made from what we can see but a substance we can't see—namely, the breath of Gods mouth: His word. The power of the Spirit of God made the world we now see and His Word continues to sustain all the universes.

The world we see today is a fallen world. But everywhere we look we see our Creator's glory. When we see the mountains or sky and say, "how beautiful!" we are declaring the beauty of His creation, whether we believe in the Creator or not. The whole world, indeed the entire universe, is a declaration of His handiwork proving to all generations throughout time that He is the Creator of all. So let us give Him the glory of which He is worthy. Even when things seem dark, He has control of all.

After the Great War in heaven the earth was left totally like a battlefield: *without form and void and darkness covered the face of the deep.* So God went to work repairing the earth, rebuilding it and making it habitable again.

He commanded, "Let there be light," and there was light, making day and night. He divided waters: air had clouds and land had springs and pools of water. He brought forth land and sea. On the earth he planted grass, herbs, seeds and trees: everything in abundance. Then he arranged the stars of heaven to give us signs of times: days, months, years and seasons. He gave us the sun to light our day and the moon to guide us at night. Then he filled the sea with all kinds of creatures. The earth he filled with an abundance of animals and the air he filled with birds and all sorts of flying creatures. The earth was full of many different kinds of living creatures and animals. The Creator was preparing everything for the prize creation of his glory: Man.

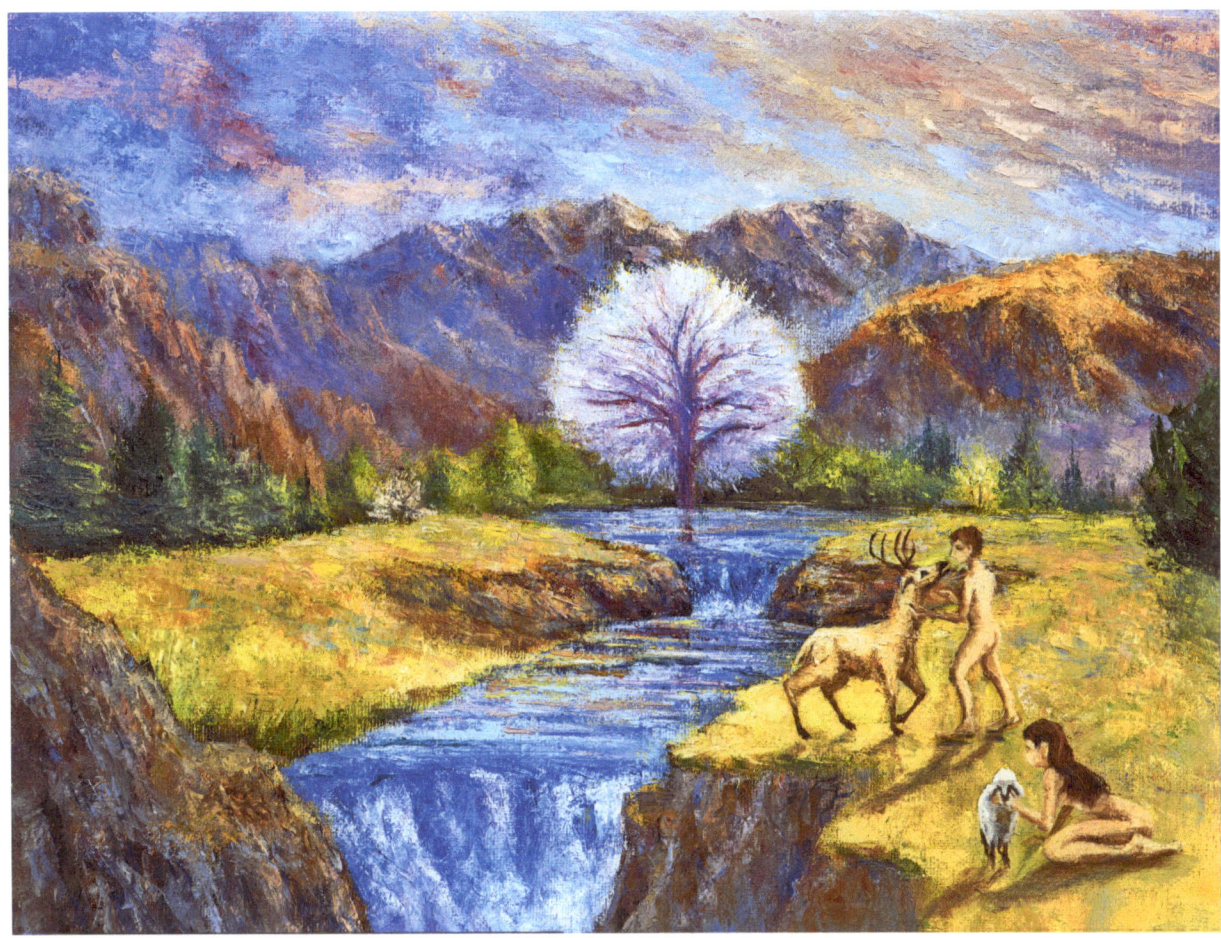

Painting 7: God made Man in His own Image

(Gen 1:27), So God created man in his own image, in the image of God created he him; male and female created he them. (Gen 2:b-6), God had not caused it to rain upon the ground. But there went up a mist from the earth and watered the whole face of the ground.

God made the Garden of Eden where He put Man: Adam and Eve. He put everything of delight there for them with all the animals and trees full of delicious fruit to eat. He also put a special covering over them of innocence so they felt no shame of being naked. God also made the earth with a special atmosphere that kept harmful rays from harming their skin and kept plenty of oxygen where their lives would be constantly renewed. They had all they needed to live forever in this state of bliss.

A Parable of the Redeemer

And God said to them…, "Have Dominion…over all the Earth."

And God blessed them and said unto them, "Be fruitful and multiply and replenish the earth and subdue it. And have dominion over the fish of the sea and over the fowl of the air and over every living thing that moves upon the earth (Gen 1:27-28).

Adam and Eve were joyous living in the wonderful garden that God had prepared especially for them. Daily they looked forward to the cool of the day when their Creator, their dearest friend, came to walk and talk with them. It was a very special time of peace, love and renewal. They knew nothing of pain, fatigue, sickness, sorrow, fear, war, struggle, guilt, shame or any other kind of hardship or evil. They had all anyone could ever long for.

Being completely ignorant of evil or danger, God warned them: *"Of every tree of the garden you may freely eat: But of the tree of the knowledge of good and evil, you shall not eat of it: for in the day that you eat thereof you shall surely die (Gen 2:16-17).*

Sometime later, as usual their Creator arrived to the garden in the cool of the day. This day He was carrying something different, a document written by His own hand giving them dominion over the earth. They were overjoyed that God would entrust them with the responsibility of dominion over such a beautiful part of His creation.

With blessing always comes responsibility! *To whom much is given much is required.* The Creator once again made very clear their responsibility: To follow his one and only command to the very letter: *"Of every tree of the garden you may freely eat: But of the tree of the knowledge of good and evil, you shall not eat of it: for in the day that you eat thereof you shall surely die.*

"That seems easy enough," they assumed. "We're already doing that," they replied confidently. In their total innocence, fear and evil were completely unknown to Adam and Eve. They were unaware that the Creator's adversary, Lucifer, disguised as a serpent, was lurking just out of sight, planning his counter attack. He was studying their weaknesses; waiting for the chance to destroy the Creator's newest creation: man.

Have you ever wondered why God doesn't bless you with what you ask for? Ask yourself, "Am I ready for the demands of this blessing's responsibility?"

The Temptation and the Fall

(Gen 2:15-17) The LORD God took the man, and put him into the Garden of Eden to dress it and to keep it. (Gen 3:1) Now the serpent was more subtle than any beast of the field which the LORD God had made. And he said unto the woman, "Has God indeed said, 'You shall not eat of every tree of the garden?'"

Life continued in the garden of bliss till one day, Lucifer, the Creator's adversary, taking the form of a serpent, came and presented himself to Eve. He knew that Adam was the first created and the woman had been taken from his side. Therefore, he knew Adam was the one with authority and should be avoided. So he slyly began making friends with Eve. He spoke beautiful words, full of wisdom, so profoundly that they went straight to her heart. "Words had never been spoken like his—so insightful and intuitive," Eve reasoned. His words began to woo her devotion. The serpent planned to gain her confidence, and then lead her astray! Subtly he laid a foundation of trust, while he searched out her weaknesses.

One day, in the depth of their conversation, he tested Eve to see how his style was working by saying, "I believe in God, too, but I would never trust him." She was taken aback by such words against her Creator! "How could you say such a thing?" she retorted. At the same time, she reasoned to herself, "All his words have been very wise—they speak directly to my heart." In fact, Lucifer's words were satisfying an increasing need she'd felt since spending time with him.

11

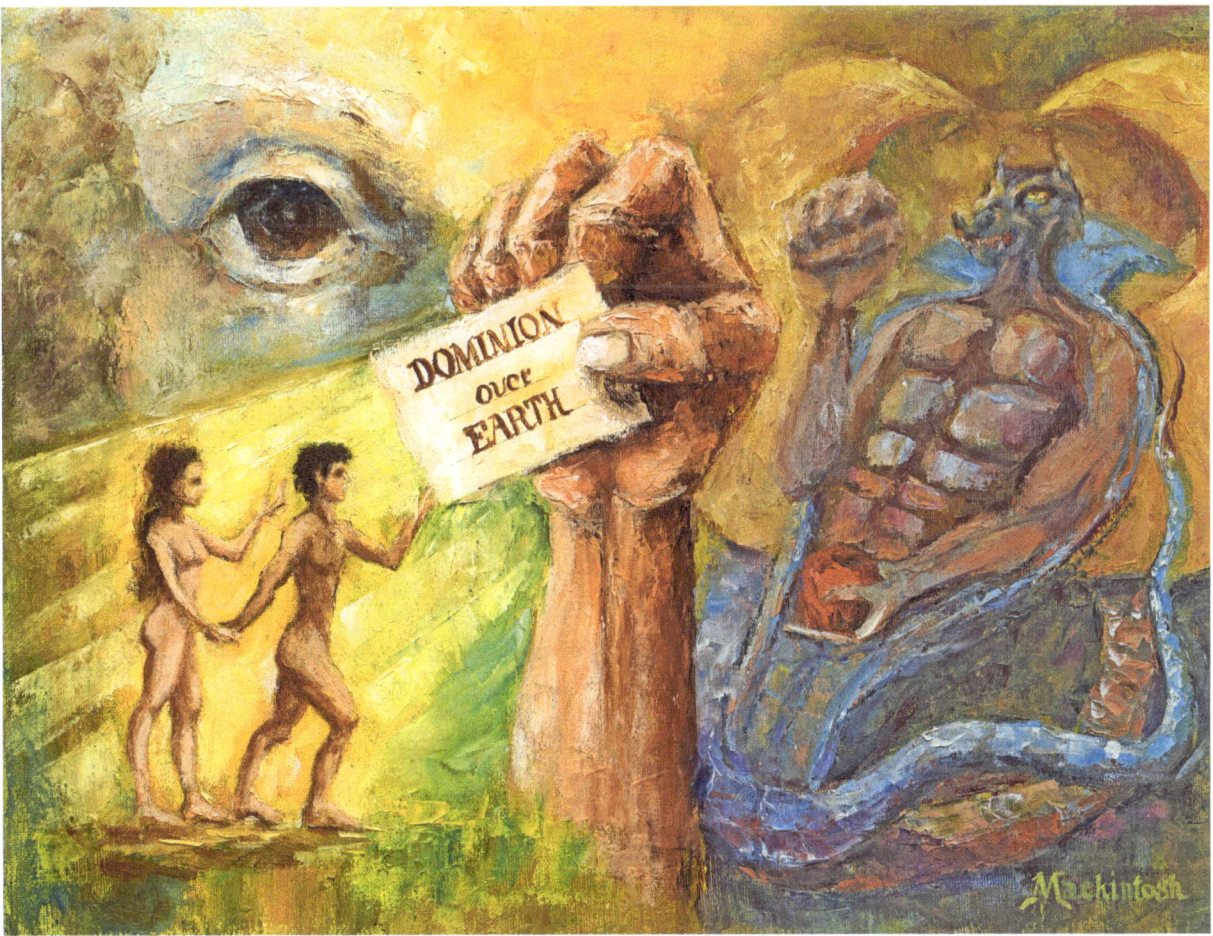

Painting 8: Have Dominion …."

Eve told Adam of her encounter with the serpent. He sternly warned her to beware of any words spoken against their Creator. She knew her husband was right and determined to avoid him, but she really missed him. "Maybe he didn't really mean what he said," she argued to herself, as memories of their precious moments occupied her thoughts. Eve revisited how special she felt as his words touched the depth of her being. She felt special and attractive with him. "He makes me feel alive. I need that!" She argued. "How can someone so good and wise be of any danger?" she contested, while wrestling with her thoughts. Eve finally decided that her new friend couldn't be evil; he was too wise for that. "Besides," she determined, "My feelings are too strong to let go of him now. I want to be free to do what I feel."
With that, a sense of liberation swept over her. She decided to live in the freedom she felt.

Every morning after that, she and her new friend ran off to have fun and play together, while Adam attended to his normal daily duties: doing the garden and caring for the animals. Day by day the serpent gained more of Eve's trust. Little by little he planted seeds of doubt about the Creator's character. Slowly she opened her heart and mind to his beautiful words. More and more Lucifer weakened her trust in her Creator by introducing more and more lies against him till Eve actually began to doubt his word.

When the serpent saw that Eve's confidence in the Creator had weakened sufficiently, he asked her, "Did God really say that you can't eat of the fruit of that certain tree?" Eve knew what her Creator had said, and answered, "We can't eat of it or even touch it lest we surely die."

The serpent responded, "You won't surely die! I've known the Creator a long time and he has no intention of letting you die. Listen to me. The tree of the knowledge of good and evil is not forbidden. That's just a myth that the Creator made up to keep you from becoming wise like Him." She knew she should run but stayed to listen just a little longer. As Eve listened, the serpent's words began to sink in. The deceiver continued. "He doesn't want you to have the level of knowledge that He has." "Wow," Eve thought, "That really makes a lot of sense," she rationalized. "His words are truly wise. He really has it all figured out." She analyzed, "It's good to be so close to someone so knowledgeable," she thought. Then she reached up to take the forbidden fruit from the serpent's hand.

The deception finally took. The serpent's lies seduced Eve away from her Creator's word and she fell into temptation. As she bit into the forbidden fruit a rush of exhilaration came over her. This was sheer pleasure.

Far away Adam was working in the fruit orchard. An ominous sense began spreading over the garden as foreboding filled the air. Anxiety gripped his soul. Fear pierced his senses like a knife. He fell from his ladder to the ground. Something new and terrible was happening. Pulling himself up he saw Eve approaching. Her countenance and body had changed. She was naked! Dread struck him like a millstone and again he fell to the ground. He knew the Creator's command was true. Death was spreading upon the earth.

Adam began to panic. He struggled to gather his wits but his senses were shattered. He knew that Eve's sin meant death. He would be alone without her. "What can I do?" he kept questioning. He loved her more than anything and now death would take her. Finally, as he considered his options, he could only think of the agony of life without her. His love for her was so deep that he decided that dying with her would be better than living without her. He would join her in death.

Eve, still giddy with her new-found freedom, and the pleasure of her sin, didn't notice Adam's distress and boldly offered him the fruit, saying, "This is the sweetest fruit in the garden, and it definitely imparts wisdom." Understanding that breaking God's law meant sure death for them both, Adam joined Eve in sin. He listened to her offer and took the fruit and ate of it also.

Idolatry enters when our love for a creature is greater than our love for our Creator. How often do we value the Creator's gifts more than our Creator? How often when we should run from temptation do we stay a little longer till the temptation overtakes us? We question, "How can this little piece of fruit bring death? Would a loving, compassionate God allow this? He always forgives so I'll try anything once."

Indeed our Creator is loving, forgiving and merciful. That's why he sets boundaries: for our protection. Crossing those boundaries brings us consequences greater than we estimate. Adam and Eve may have enjoyed the fruit while it was in their mouth, but the results were deadly. Their disobedience brought the curses of sin, death, nakedness, shame, guilt, hatred and war into the whole world, from which we all still suffer. Yet, our hope is in our Redeemer.

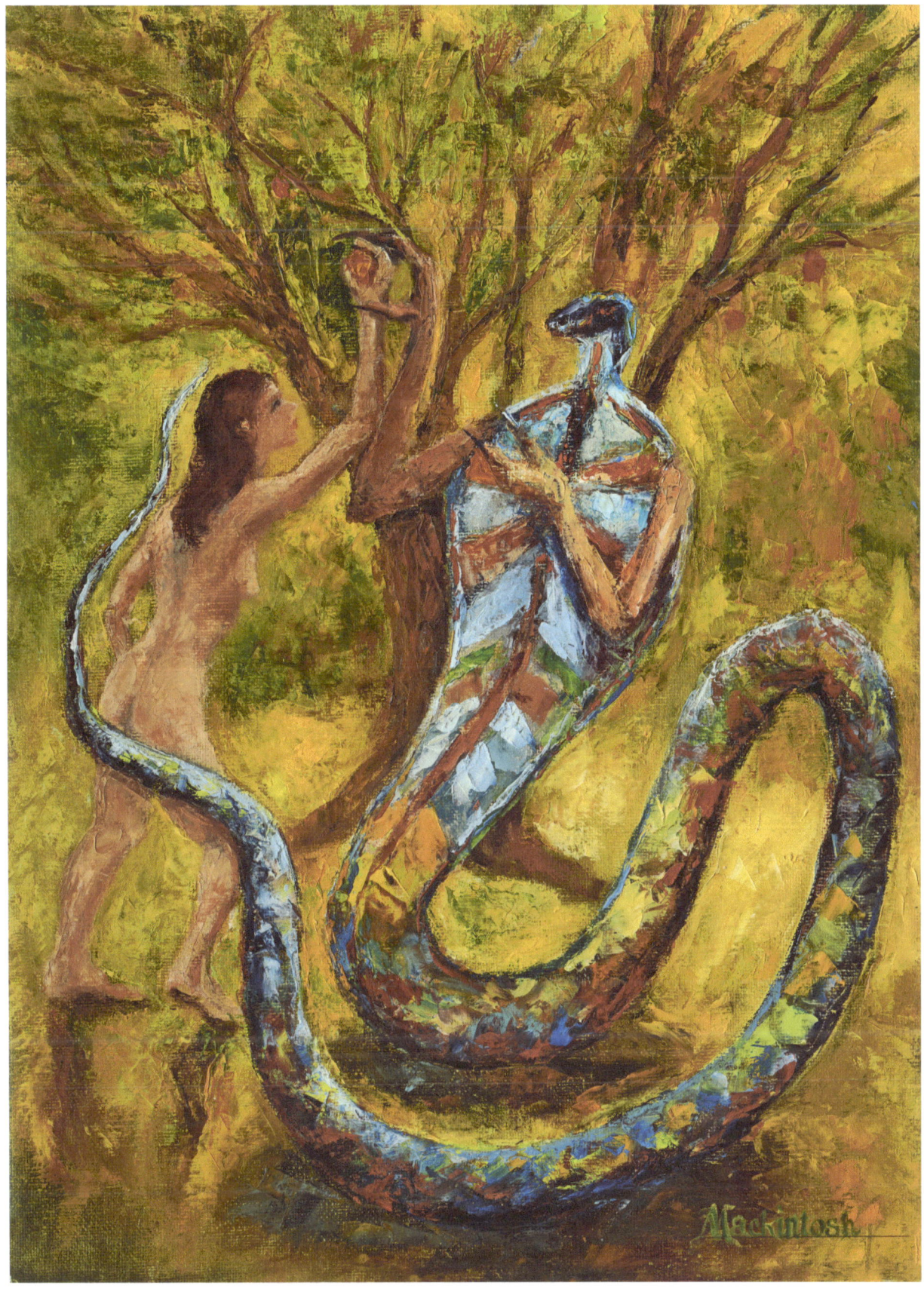

Painting 9: The Temptation and the Fall

The Blood Sacrifice

(Gen 3:21) Unto Adam also and to his wife did the LORD God make coats of skins, and clothed them.

Immediately, death spread over the garden. Sin's guilt pierced like a knife blade deeply into Adam and Eve's heart. Sorrow hit them like a weight they'd never known. As they realized the magnitude of their sin, conflicts and accusations heated up between them to the point of hatred. All of their love turned to bitterness. They suddenly stopped, looked at each other and questioned, "Is this the knowledge we were seeking?" Their love and harmony was gone. Strife, hatred and bitterness had replaced it. These were new and evil feelings. They examined their circumstances and saw that evil was now very present; the good they'd known was disappearing. Adam's love for his beloved Eve was embittered because she'd tempted him. She felt guilt for having been deceived. "Is this the death our Creator warned us about?" they questioned. This was worse than they had imagined. Lies of the adversary had enticed them into disobedience and the results were terrible: a life of living death.

The sun was fading as the cool of the day approached. They struggled to find a remedy but their wisdom had abandoned them. Panicking, they questioned, "What shall we do?" as they grasped for lucidity. "How can we face the Creator with this guilt, nakedness and shame?" they questioned. A cover-up was the answer. That was the quickest and easiest way. So they sewed fig leaves together and made aprons.

God saw right through their cover-up. His heart welled up with compassion as He looked upon their futile efforts. The heartache He felt over losing their love immediately turned into grace, which poured like a flood from His heart, covering their sin from His eyes. Our Redeemer had the answer.

He knew the grave consequences of their disobedience: that it brought death to His whole creation. Everyone, from that moment forward, would be born into an atmosphere of sin, death and destruction.

So God took of the lambs they had loved and cared for and as they watched, He shed the blood of those animals. The life's blood of those animals covered their sin (made atonement) from the Creator's sight. Life of all flesh is in its blood. He exchanged the life of the animals they loved so that they could continue living. This sacrifice was needed to redeem Adam and Eve from the jaws of immediate death. It was also needed to remit the curse of the ground and to restore them to their Creator, the source of life. Their innocence, which had protected them, was forever gone: they were naked. God took the skins of the sacrificed animals and made clothing to cover their nakedness.

They were no longer allowed to remain in the protection of their beloved garden. The atonement had abated God's anger, but death now polluted the earth. They now needed more than ever the friendship of their Redeemer.

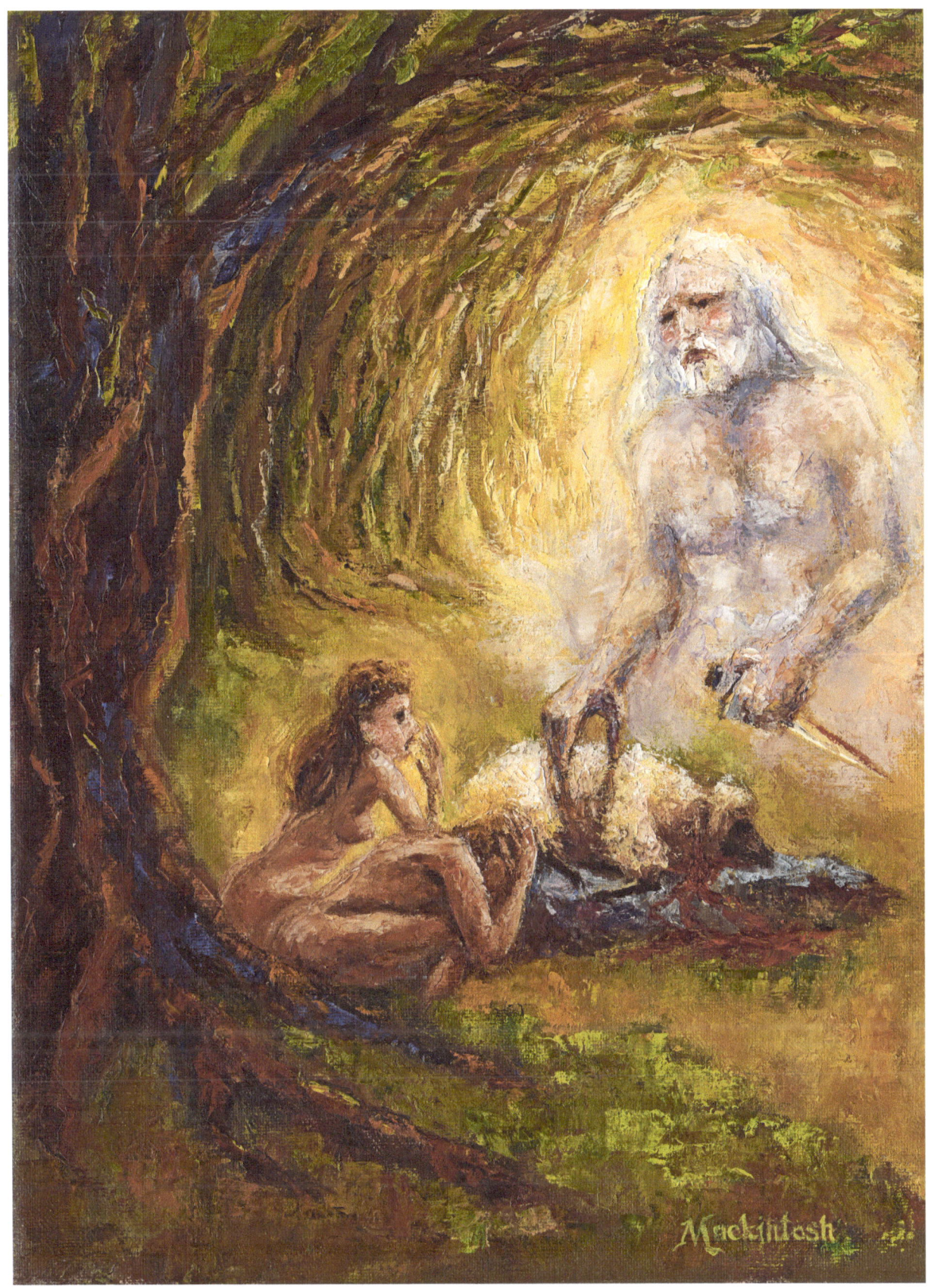

Painting 10: The Blood Sacrifice

Chapter 3: The Cursed New World

Expelled from the Garden

(Gen 3:24) So he drove out the man; and he placed at the east of the Garden of Eden, Cherubim, with a flaming sword which turned every way, to keep them away from the tree of life.

At every turn our first parents' sin relentlessly pursued them. Their broken fellowship with their Creator had grave consequences. Eve's sorrow would be multiplied in child birth. The ground was cursed with thorns and thistles, forcing Adam to sweat and work hard to provide bread for them. Then the Lord cursed the serpent: *And the Lord God said unto the serpent, "Because you have done this you are cursed above...every beast of the field.... And I will put enmity between thee and the woman, and between thy seed and her seed. It shall bruise thy head and thou shall bruise his heel," (Geneses 3:14, 15).* Within the curse upon the serpent, there is a promise made to the woman: *that from her seed (her offspring) God would provide the* Redeemer, to save man from his sin and death. The serpent (Lucifer) would strike the Redeemer's heel but the Redeemer would crush the serpent's head.

Then the Creator drove them out from the garden. Conditions outside the garden were harsh. Suffering one chastisement after another, they reeled from God's scourging. Now they faced a world of curses, thorns and thistles, futility, bereft of hope and separation from their Creator. They ran into the wilderness dreading that God's fierce anger would strike again.

Fear and sorrow seized their heart, as they wandered without direction into the desolation. There was no way for them to live out here. "Surely," they rationalized, "God has sent us out here to die." A chill came over them as the sun dipped closer to the horizon. A light breeze chilled them even more as it brushed against their tears. They needed protection so they fashioned a small shelter of branches with a grassy floor. Little comfort was theirs as they lay themselves down, their eyes swollen shut from tears of hopelessness. Exhausted from fear, sleep finally overtook them but their dreams were filled with the terror of God's wrath.

The morning sun gave Adam and Eve little hope. They had made it through the first night but things were foreboding. Death was lurking. When and where would it strike? They found some berries to eat, but nothing compared to the garden. They spent the whole day searching out what little food there was, all the while trying to avoid thorns that carpeted the ground, which pierced their flesh with every step. The berries they sought were completely sheltered by thorns. Thorns of the cursed ground were everywhere, piercing their hands and feet, demanding their life's blood as recompense, for yielding its fruit. After several hours the sun got hot and began to burn them, unlike the garden.

They sought out some shade, sat down to rest and mend their bleeding wounds. Reviewing again all that had happened, especially how terrifying God was, they wondered, "Will we ever again be able to talk with him?" They were terrified of him. Though harsh and accusing words had also passed between them Adam and Eve found, as they talked, that their love for each other was still strong. All they had was each other. If they could stay alive, that would be enough. Love covers a multitude of sins. Then they questioned, "All has been cursed but love still remains. Is it possible that our Creator still loves us?"

Adam and Eve, terrified and perplexed, continued their journey of survival. Recovering would take time. As time passed, hunger pushed them further out into their thorny domain where they hoped to expand their diminishing food supply. The once friendly animals were now competitors. They were faster, more agile and better at reaching the precious fruit, which made survival more difficult. Some animals feared them but others were ferocious. Some ate their competitors, fighting to the death for food.

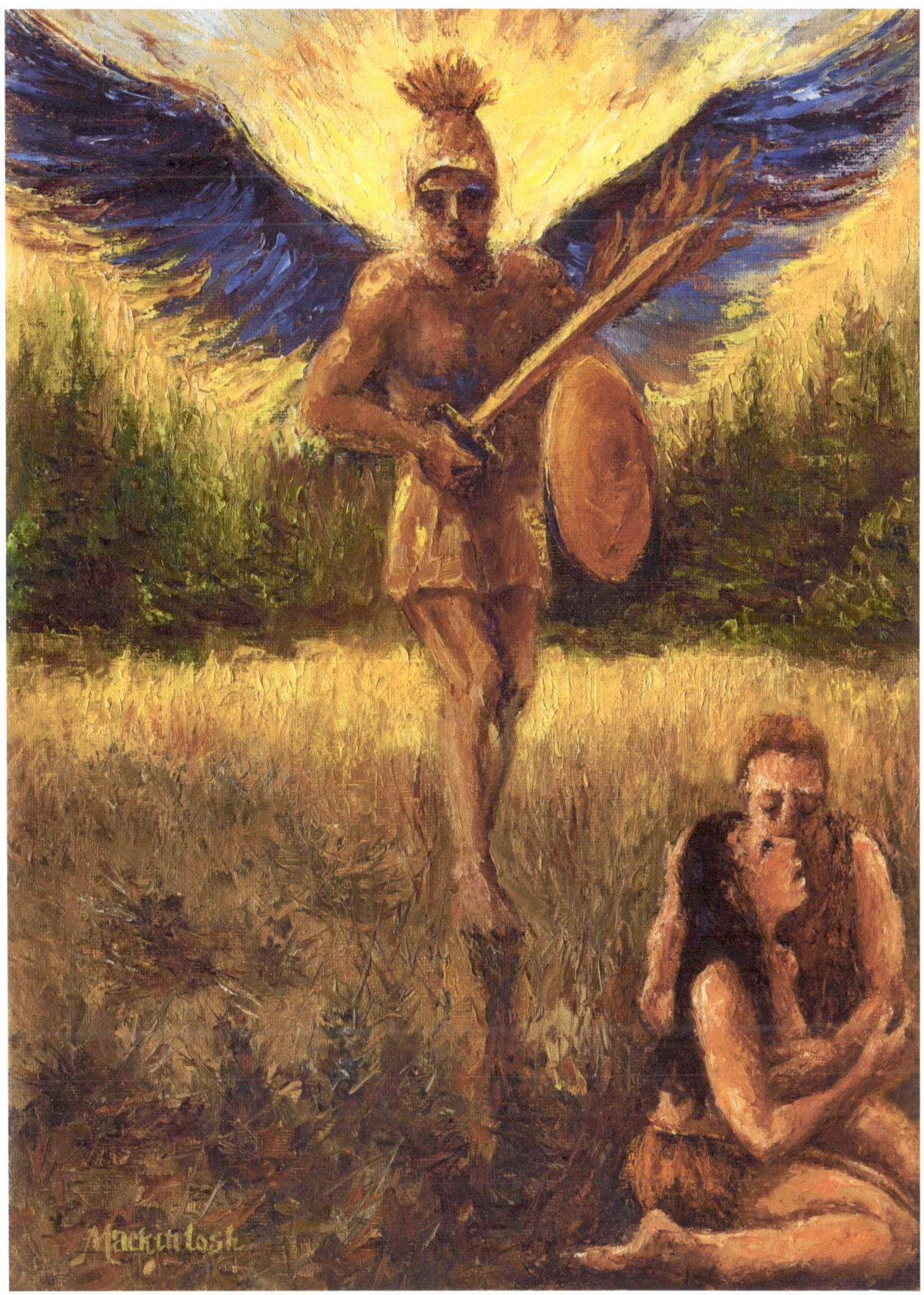

Painting 11: Expelled from the Garden

Death was everywhere. The peace they knew in the garden was gone. They longed for the wonderful garden they so foolishly exchanged for this thorn field. With no knowledge of survival they longed for the wisdom of their Creator's counsel. "If we could talk with Him as before…," they thought. "But our sin is so great. How can we reach Him?" They agreed together that they needed Him. But sin was so devastating and he was so far away. Adam, though still terrified, realized that the Creator was the source of all, including Eve. She was His gift to him. But he needed to put his love for his Creator before all.

Fear began to grow in Adam and Eve as the following weeks introduced colder weather. The fruit they relied on was vanishing. They also needed a shelter that would withstand the cold. Till now, they had barely survived. Now, with harsh weather coming and supplies scarce, they saw more and more need for their Creator's knowledge and wisdom. Whom else could they call? Who had been their only true friend? They finally concluded, "our Creator is all we have."

Though not recovered from the trauma of God's wrath, things were getting desperate. Shivering together in their cold hut as snow mounted outside, they decided, "He may slay us, or He may save us. We're dying here. Why not appeal to His mercy?" So in humility they called out to their Creator for mercy from the depths their hearts, "O Lord" they cried out into the cold night, "If we could only see you and talk with you again. But how can we since our sin is so great? You rightly put us out here alone in this wilderness of thorns and thistles, and now we are freezing in this snow for sinning against you. We remembered somewhere that you are our Redeemer, so we call on you now. Will you leave us here to die? You, Lord, are all we have! We know of no other Creator or friend but you, our Savior. Save us! We are destitute sinners in need of your salvation. Be our Redeemer!"

In my own experience, sometimes the Lord's chastening seemed too much to bear. I've been angry and proud and resisted calling on Him. But when I saw that He was all I had and called on Him, He answered me with mercy and redemption. Tenderly but firmly, He restores us to Himself, teaching us wisdom and prudence and how to avoid future troubles. He is our Redeemer

Cain and Abel

(Gen 4:2) And Abel was a keeper of sheep, but Cain was a tiller of the ground.

As time passed, Adam and Eve learned to trust their Creator more and more. He came to them in their desolate wilderness with words of love and compassion. He healed their wounds and spoke peace to their affliction and kindness to their distresses. He taught them to make shelters and clothing from lamb's wool, to hunt and fish, the proper seasons to cultivate the earth to make it bear fruit from plants, seeds and trees. Although the ground was cursed, they saw that having God's blessings brought forth abundantly for everyone. They had children and their children had children and their families flourished and grew into great communities.

Adam and Eve began to enjoy their life now mainly because they learned to depend on their Creator who had become also their Redeemer. They drew closer to Him, loving Him more deeply than ever before. He taught them wisdom from His treasure of knowledge. Adam learned to carry out his duty as priest of his family. Eve learned to commit the complexities of her life to the Redeemer, and taught her children to do the same. Their Redeemer's words comforted and healed them from the pain, strife and the guilt of their sin. He taught them to live in peace, harmony and forgiveness in their now cursed world.

They longed to spend time with their Redeemer, who had saved them from the scourge of death. Setting aside the seventh day for rest and worship of their Creator, they gained from Him wisdom, counsel and learned to walk in peace.

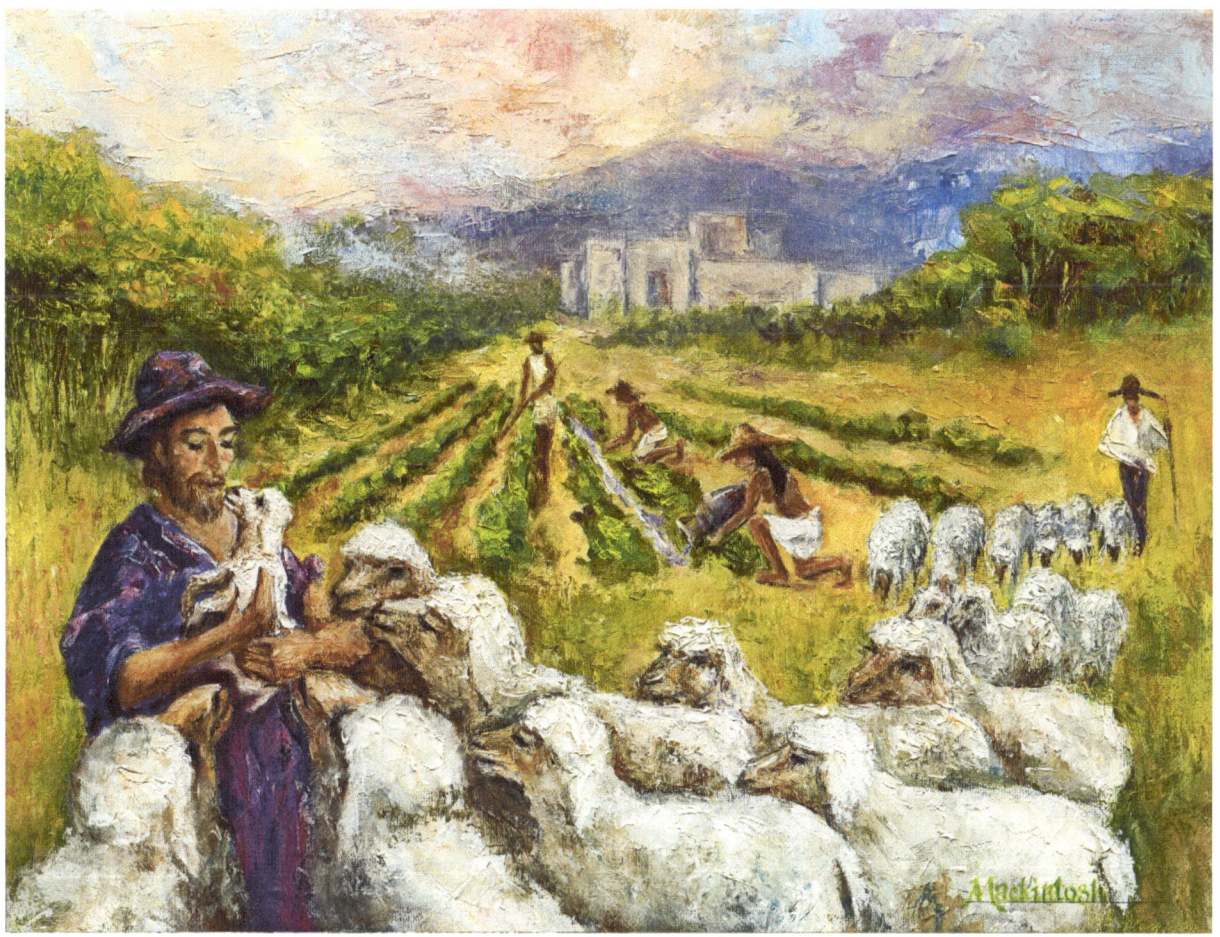

Painting 12: Cain and Abel

One hundred thirty years passed and the Creator's abundant blessings on Adam, Eve and their children were apparent. He supplied their needs, which by now made up a very large community indeed. All those years Adam and Eve had babies. Their babies had babies and all had families. That's 130 years of babies having babies. Of all those, two names: Cain and Abel, Adam and Eve's first sons, stand out. Cain tilled the ground, and Abel tended sheep.

With God's blessings multiplied to them, all were quite happy with life, enjoying the gifts God gave them. Then one day, as the story goes, Abel's sheep got into Cain's field of vegetables, eating and destroying much of his crop. Cain was livid. "After all the work I did, your stupid sheep had to come and destroy all my efforts," he yelled. But Abel protested, "You, brother, should be more lenient. You use their wool for clothing and enjoy their meat for food. And besides, haven't I always made it up to you when something like this happens? Cut me some slack."

That is not what Cain wanted to hear, although, he had no idea what the right answer should be. "Abel purposely turned a blind eye to his sheep and allowed them to get into my field. This could have been prevented. It's unforgivable," Cain grumbled under his breath. "He's going to pay for this," he promised.

This wasn't the first time Cain had been unforgiving. He had become increasingly short tempered over the years. The community noticed but concluded, "That's just the way he is." A few days prior, his neighbor's dog barked all night leaving Cain beside himself with fatigue. The community council was called to consider the matter. Abel was esteemed by all as a wise peacemaker, so they asked his advice. For Abel, this was simply a matter of the neighbor feeding

20

and watering his dog before bed, and for Cain to just put in earplugs. The community all agreed. But Cain couldn't release it, stating, "Nothing will make up for my loss of sleep. I should be reimbursed for that as well."

Living close to people was becoming increasingly difficult for Cain. He simply couldn't release things and demanded compensation for every small and petty thing. Over the years these grudges mounted. Tension was building to the point that he would explode at the slightest provocation. If only he had learned to give it all to his Redeemer.

The Two Different Offerings

(Gen 4:3-5) And in process of time it came to pass, that Cain brought of the fruit of the ground an offering unto the LORD. And Abel, also brought of the firstlings of his flock and of the fat thereof. And the LORD had respect unto Abel and to his offering: But unto Cain and to his offering he had not respect.

From their parents, Cain and Abel, and all Adam's children, learned God's law: once every year he required the blood of a spotless animal to be shed to make atonement (a covering) for sin. This yearly rite was to cover man's sin from the Creator's sight, which was necessary to re-establish fellowship with him for the following year. This was also necessary for the Creator's blessing to continue on them and their community.

As Adam's children grew and formed their own families, each father would take on the priestly duty of making the sacrifice for his own family. From the first year Adam and Eve were evicted from the garden, this rite continued unbroken for one hundred and thirty years. Adam and Eve's family had carried out their Redeemer's command faithfully.

Cain, a farmer who worked the land, had traded his fruits and vegetables with Abel, a shepherd, for a lamb to offer up to the Lord. But this year Cain was still bitter with Abel for allowing his sheep to invade his field. The damage had been too great to forgive. The more he thought about it the angrier he got. "This year God will have to be satisfied with vegetables," he decided. "Besides, they're just as good as a lamb. Really, what difference does it make?"

Adam, his father, warned him that God would not accept vegetables as an offering. It must be a blood sacrifice in order to remit sin and hold back death's cure from them. In fact, vegetables might even offend God since He had cursed the ground. Blood was needed to keep that curse from entering and that the earth remain fruitful. Cain responded to Adam, "Yeah, yeah, yeah, I know, I've heard all that for the past hundred and thirty years and I'm fed up with it. Anyway, I don't believe that rot. That's just a bunch of myths to keep us all under your control. Just get off my back." With that he left to do his own will and not God's will.

He offered to God vegetables from his garden and Abel offered up to the Creator a perfect lamb. God accepted Abel's sacrifice but had no respect for Cain's. Why would he want to offend his Redeemer?

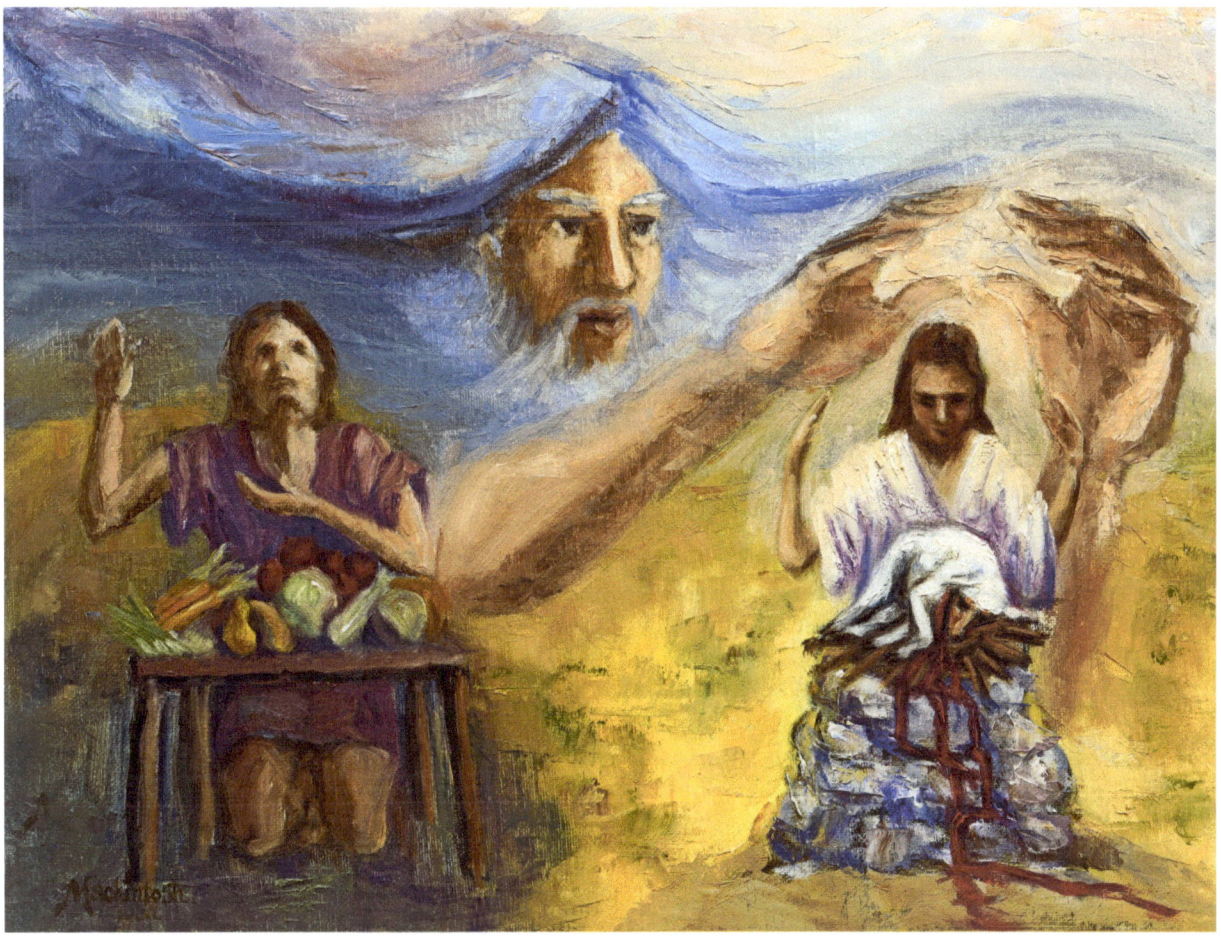

Painting 13: The Two Different Offerings

Cain was Enraged

(Gen 4: 5-7) Cain was very enraged, and his countenance fell. And the LORD said unto Cain, Why are you enraged? Why is thy countenance fallen? If you do well, shall ye not be accepted? And if ye do not well, sin lay at the door….

Cain, full of rage, returned to his house shouting out his displeasure with God's rejection of his offering. He was even more outraged that God had respected Abel's. He continued venting his hatred for Abel his brother.

The community knew that when Cain went on one of his rages, it was best to just hide out until he calmed down. So they all disappeared. "If I could get back at God for this I would," he screamed. "But that's impossible because he's God and I'm just a man," he stated. "I deserve better than being treated as second class. I'll have my revenge against him and against Abel somehow," he promised.

Adam, hearing the commotion, came out to soothe his son with his words of truth and wisdom. His mother, Eve, brought him a bowl of his favorite vegetable soup, hoping to quiet him. Cain settled a little listening to his father's words hoping for absolution.

Adam proceeded with gentle words of peace, full of wisdom to calm Cain's soul. He encouraged Cain to relinquish malice and pursue peace, abandon vengeance and search out the Redeemer's mercy. Cain sat there filtering through all his father's words hoping for vindication. Adam continued, "The fruit of the ground we eat for health, the flesh of beasts we eat for strength. Their blood, we pour into the ground to remit sin's curse so that the earth will continue to bring forth her fruit. The blood of the lamb remits sin from us, whether committed by us or against us. Learn forgiveness and you will gain freedom, clarity and wisdom."

Then Adam recommended, "The best solution is to just offer up a lamb in obedience to God's command." At that, Cain's fury unleashed like a flood drowning out his father's words. "Don't you understand?" he roared. "I hate Abel." "How can you expect me to do business with that slime after he and the community cheated me out of all my profits? He purposely let his stinky sheep into my field?" he protested. "I want nothing more to do with him, ever!" Cain bellowed, as he stormed from Adam's presence. Raging at full volume he ranted, "Getting an animal from Abel is out of the question." Shouting at an ear piercing level for all to hear he said, "I hate Abel more now than I ever have."

As he shuffled back out to his field he sarcastically mumbled, "How could my father, who is said to be so wise, come up with such senseless words?" Soon he found comfort plowing the ground he loved. The smell of fresh earth turning over soothed his soul and refreshed his spirit. But before he knew it, however, his anger had rekindled and he continued seething over the grievous injustice. He hashed the situation over again seeking defense for his position.

The LORD met up with Cain as he was plowing the field, and said unto Cain, *"Why are you so enraged? Why is thy countenance fallen?" If you do well, shall you not be accepted? And if you do not well, sin lay at the door...."* God tried to persuade Cain to release his anger, change his mind, to return and make things right. And more importantly, to be obedient before his Redeemer.

But the adversary was there stealing away God's word, offering instead words he wanted to hear. Whispering in his ear, the adversary spoke, "You deserve better than this. Look at how God disgraced you in front of everybody. I know how you can get back at Abel and God too." This got Cain's attention. The adversary continued, "Just kill Abel. That will strip God of his pride and glory, and you will avenge yourself against Abel." "How so?" inquired Cain. The adversary continued, "Because God loves and honors Abel above everyone on the earth. Abel is always faithful. With him dead, everyone will see that honoring God is futile, that curses will be the reward for their faithfulness. That way, God will be stripped of power, and his honor tarnished. The truth of his glory will be revealed as a lie and his word as deception. They will abandon their trust of him."

Although Cain knew he was doing the adversary's bidding, the satisfaction of vengeance thrilled him. So he and Lucifer set out to invent a scheme to get rid of Abel, his brother. Cain rejected the words of his Redeemer.

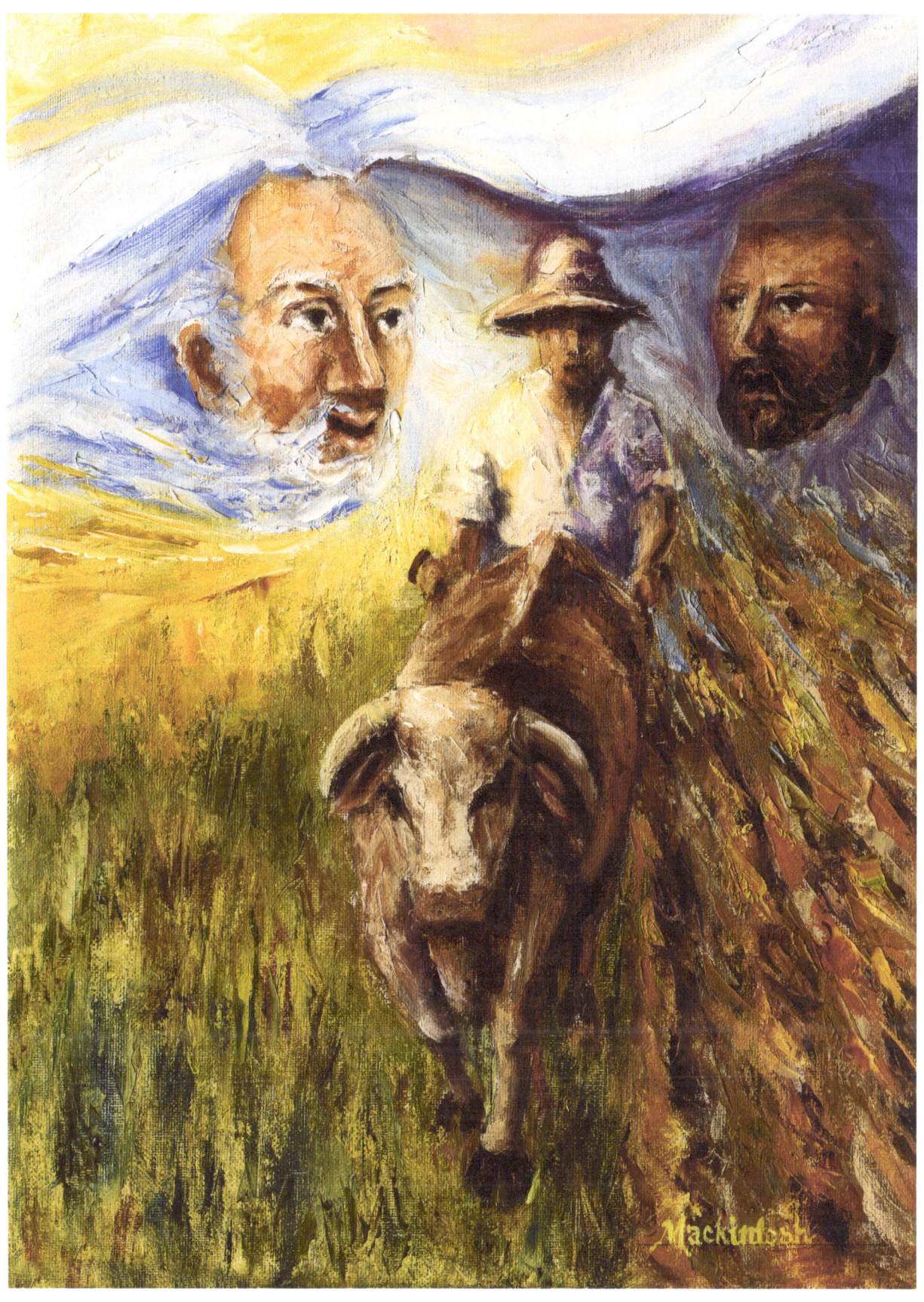

Painting 14: Cain was Enraged

A Parable of the Redeemer

The First Murder

(Gen 4:8) And Cain talked with Abel his brother: and it came to pass, when they were in the field, that Cain rose up against Abel his brother, and slew him.

As Cain planned the treachery, his hatred for Abel turned to obsession, pressing him on, fixating his sentiments on revenge. "Then, and only then, will I be vindicated for the way God insulted me," he analyzed. "Then, and only then, will accounts be settled with Abel's injustice against me." Continuing on, "He only paid me what the council agreed on," he reviewed. "But his sheep did more damage than they were willing to admit. Now he will pay. This will be a lesson he won't forget—it will be final."

Before long, Cain had a plan that would work. He sent a messenger to his brother Abel with a note, saying, "Dear brother Abel, let our strife end. Have mercy lest I die. For my flesh deprives me of repose and my body aches with fatigue, sleep is a stranger to my eyes and slumber leaves me weary. Meet me, I pray you, out in this certain field privately, away from seeing eyes, hearing ears and mouths that speak lying gossip. Speak with me, brother, for compassion's sake, that we may gain a resolution. Discord's burden permits me no rest. Let's have an end to this that I may again have peace, Your brother, Cain."

Abel was overjoyed with his brother's note. Peace was what he always wanted. And now his big brother wanted to mend their rift. Abel was so happy he thought the breeze would float him away. With eagerness he made haste going out to meet his brother.

But Cain's heart was deceitful: he rose up and killed his brother. Whenever ancient barriers are broken down, the curses they restrain will enter society like a flood. Murder entered. But still our Creator is our Redeemer.

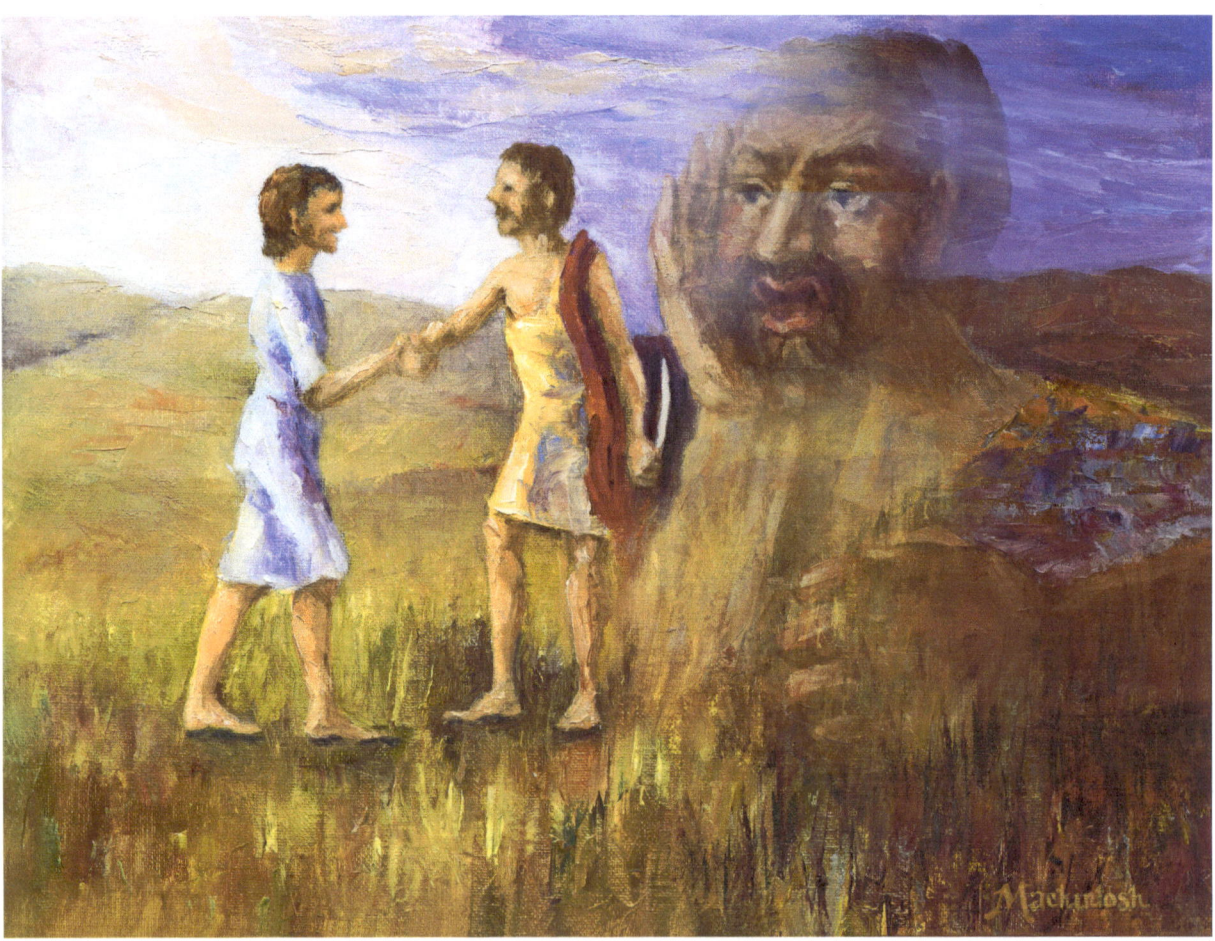

Painting 15: The First Murder

Chapter 4: The Wages of Sin

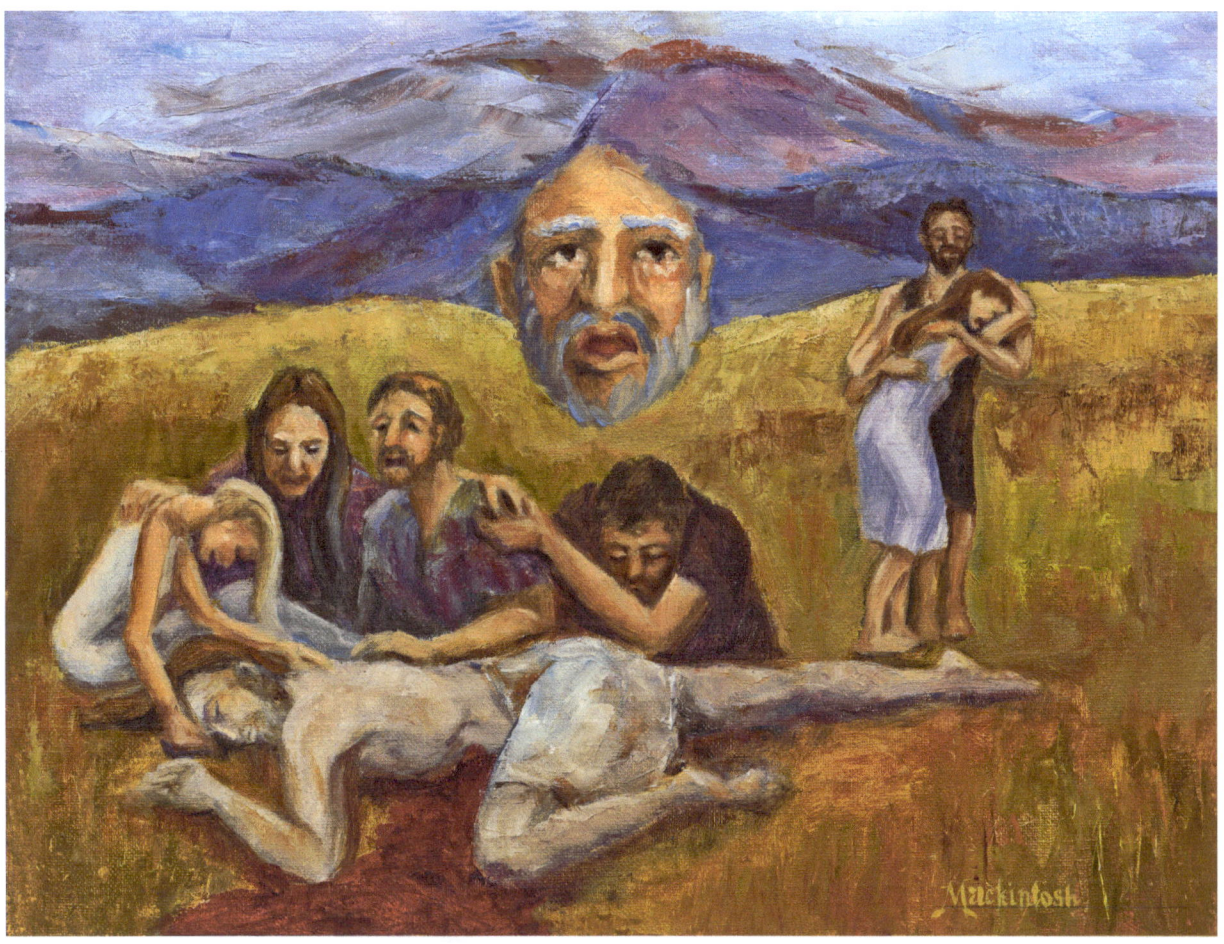

Painting 16: The Grief of Death

(Gen 4:9) And the LORD said unto Cain," Where is Abel thy brother?" And he said," I know not: Am I my brother's keeper?" And he said, "What have you done?" "The voice of thy brother's blood cries unto me from the ground."

Everyone gathered to grieve the loss of Abel with Adam and Eve. Everyone loved Abel because he loved them with impartiality. He was a wise, righteous man, a peacemaker with a loving and gentle spirit. But now out of vengeance Cain had killed him.

Adam and Eve were stricken with grief as again their society deteriorated. Abel's death devastated Eve, stripping her of hope in God's promise that from her seed would come the Redeemer to crush the serpent's head. Her hope that Abel would fulfill that promise was now dead and with it also died her hope of absolution.

Grief wrenched Eve's heart so that she despaired of life. "All my hope is gone and my expectations lost. How can I bear this," she questioned. "God, you warned us that eating the fruit brings death. But how many times, how many years must I die this death for my sin?" she sobbed. "How can we survive death's ravenous hunger?" she inquired. "Will sin never release us till we be destroyed?" she cried.

In deep distress she emptied her heart, groaning in bitterness out to her Creator. "When will you accept my repentance, expunge my account and free me from the bondage of sin and this abyss of death?" She continued, "My son Abel loved you and honored you above all else in this whole world," she protested. "And yet you killed him."

Eve's eyes poured down tears watering the seed of Abel's blood, which the earth had earlier received. God heard Eve's cry and tasted the salt of her tears in His own mouth. He also mourned Abel's death along with those in grief. His heart was rent over the death of His beloved child.

As their tears fell to the earth the seed of Abel's blood was awakened and cried from the ground. God was not deaf to the cry of His daughter Eve, nor would He be deaf to the voice of Abel's blood for vengeance. He would answer and quickly.

People of ancient times understood that the shedding of innocent blood demands retribution, which will only be satisfied by the blood of the guilty. By deceit, wicked Cain killed righteous Abel. Sin's consequence, like an unrelenting plague, has kept returning, rendering man's expectations miserable and his confidence desperate. Fear penetrated man's consciousness enslaving his soul to the knowledge that his finality is death.

The wall restraining murder was breached. Death invaded the whole world assuring that no one would get out alive. Death is the one appointment we must all keep. Still, man's only hope is his Redeemer.

A Fugitive and a Vagabond shall thou be…

(Gen 4:11-16) And now thou art cursed from the earth, which hath opened her mouth to receive thy brother's blood from thy hand; When you till the ground, it shall not henceforth yield unto thee her strength; a fugitive and a vagabond shall thou be in the earth…

And Cain said unto the LORD, My punishment is greater than I can bear…It shall come to pass, that every one that finds me shall slay me. And the LORD said unto him… whosoever slays Cain, vengeance shall be taken on him sevenfold. And the LORD set a mark upon Cain, lest …anyone should kill him. And Cain went out from the presence of the LORD, and dwelt in the land of Nod, on the east of Eden.

The ground was now cursed against Cain as the Lord declared. He chose to shed his brother's blood instead of offering the blood of a lamb acceptable to God. Now Abel's blood cried out for vengeance against him, whereas the blood of a lamb would call out for remission.

God could not allow Cain to live around people that thought he should die for killing Abel. So He drove him out of the community. He packed up his stuff, wife and family and went east of Eden toward the land of Nod. After arriving, Cain built a city. He and his wife had a son he named Enoch, after whom he also named the city.

Cain had to learn new skills of hunting and fishing, which skills he passed on to his sons. Soon Cain's family grew with children, grandchildren and great-grandchildren. They were a diligent group studying the arts, including animal husbandry, musical instruments and playing music on harps and organs. In time they developed the art of metal working, tool making and developed farm implements, which were highly sought after by surrounding communities.

Word of their new technologies spread and soon the City of Enoch attracted commerce from near and far, drawing passersby, trade caravans and those seeking to learn the knowledge of their arts and skills. The City of Enoch became known as a center of highest learning, where Tubal-Cain, the son of Lamech, the great-grandson of Cain, was the chief instructor of craftsmen. As an artificer, (one who combined the discipline of magic with craftsmanship), he taught the forging of brass and iron, and also taught all the skills of the newest technologies.

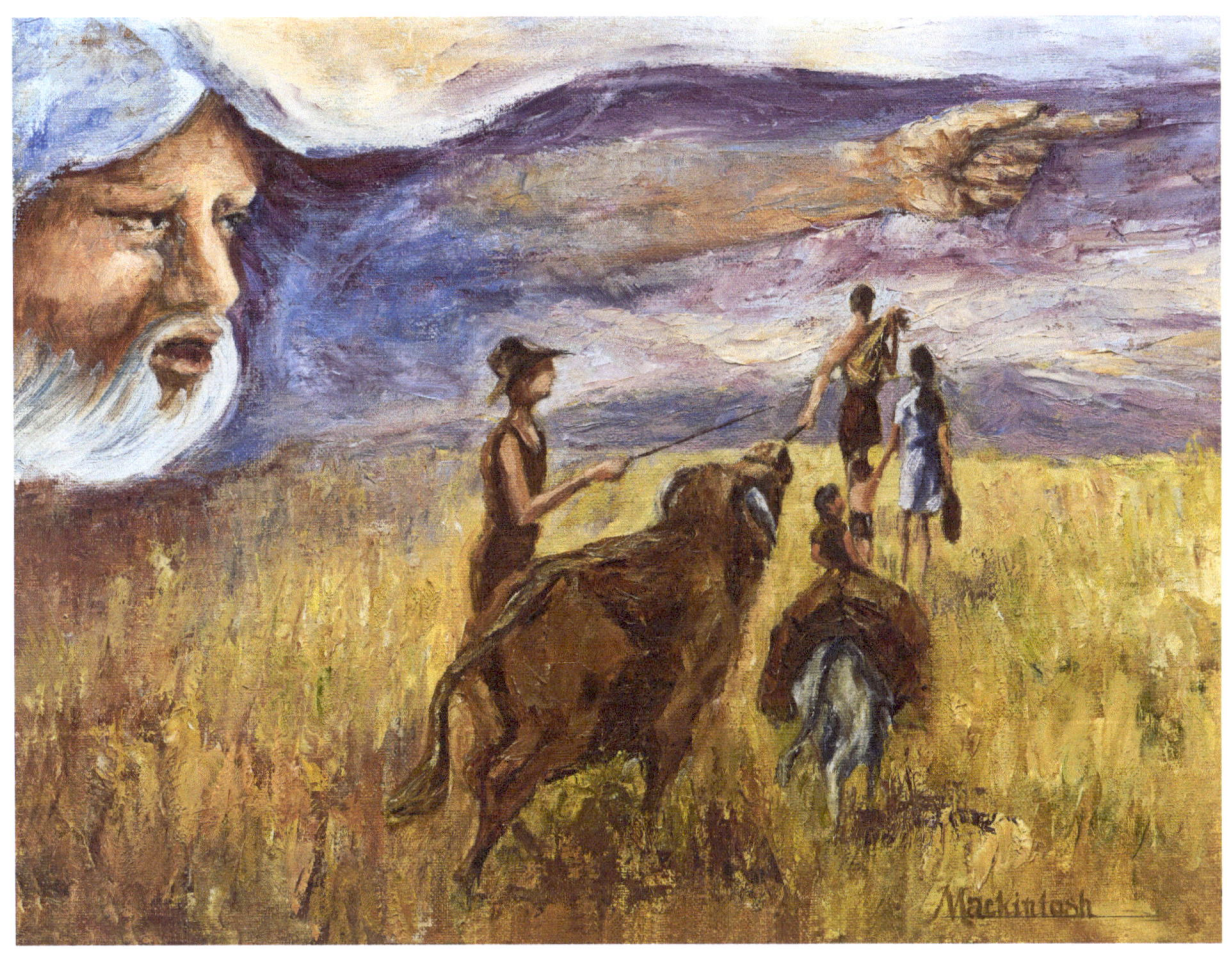

Painting 17: A Fugitive and a Vagabond…

Hunting: The Thrill of the Kill

(Genesis 4:23-24) Lamech said unto his wives, Adah and Zillah, Hear my voice; ye wives of Lamech, hearken unto my speech: for I have slain a man to my wounding .... If Cain shall be avenged sevenfold, truly Lamech seventy and sevenfold.

Tubal-Cain enjoyed hunting with his father Lamech. But his father was old, and his eyes had grown dim. So he would invite Tubal-Cain to go out with him as his spotter. Tubal-Cain also liked going out hunting to test the new arrows he'd made with tips of brass.

Lamech, though his eyes were dim, was still good at gauging distance and trajectory. So he and his son made a good team, usually successful enough to eat well.

The account goes: Lamech and his son Tubal-Cain went out hunting one morning early before sun-rise when shadows were yet purple, having only light enough to spot their game but not their game to spot them. After venturing a short distance into the wilderness, Tubal-Cain spotted what appeared to be a large deer or maybe an elk. The darkness thwarted Tubal-Cain's vision, but he could see that this animal was big and would provide enough meat for quite a while. He pointed it out to his father, Lamech who focused on the target through his dim eyes.

He, with confidence, calculated the distance, gauged the flight path of his missile and discharged the new metal-tipped arrow. As it coursed through the air, they both followed its arch as gleams of the dawning sun light danced upon the shaft. The projectile traveled directly to its objective then disappeared into the obscurity of morning shadows. Uncertain of their results, they ran up the hill with excited anticipation to survey their mark. This was what they loved about hunting: the thrill of the kill. Through dawn's light, they saw their arrow had brought down a great kill. Their excitement grew as they drew closer.

Arriving at the site, they discovered in horror that the game taken down was Cain, their great grandfather. Lamech was stricken with terror. God had put a curse on anyone that killed Cain. Now that curse was to come on him sevenfold. This was the worst day of his life.

With foreboding, Lamech returned home and told his two wives, who were also stricken with fear. They knew that if God's curse came on their house nothing would survive. So they refused to live with Lamech or even let him in the house. After a few years however, they reasoned that God's curse did not apply to hunting accidents, but revenge killing. God had heard Abel's blood crying out for vengeance against Cain and responded. (Embellished account from the Book of Jasher 2:26-30).

Be aware: Innocent blood always cries out for vengeance. *Whatever you sow, that will you also reap, (Galatians 6:7).* Just and righteous is our Redeemer.

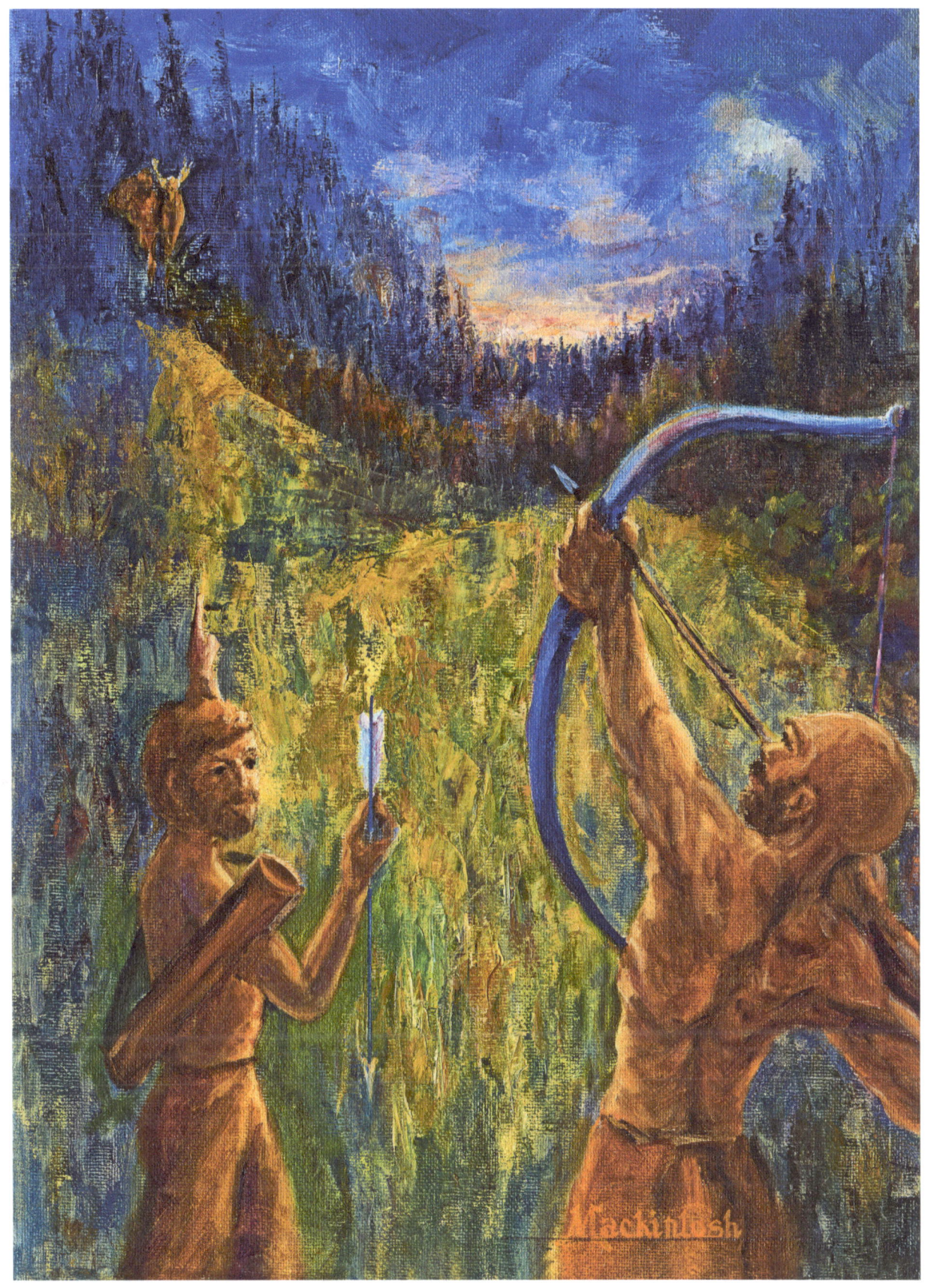

Painting 18: The Thrill of the Kill

A Parable of the Redeemer

Chapter 5: Omnipotence of the Redeemer

(Dan 4:35) And all the inhabitants of the earth are reputed as nothing: and he does according to his will in the army of heaven, and among the inhabitants of the earth: and none can stay his hand, or say unto him, What are you doing?

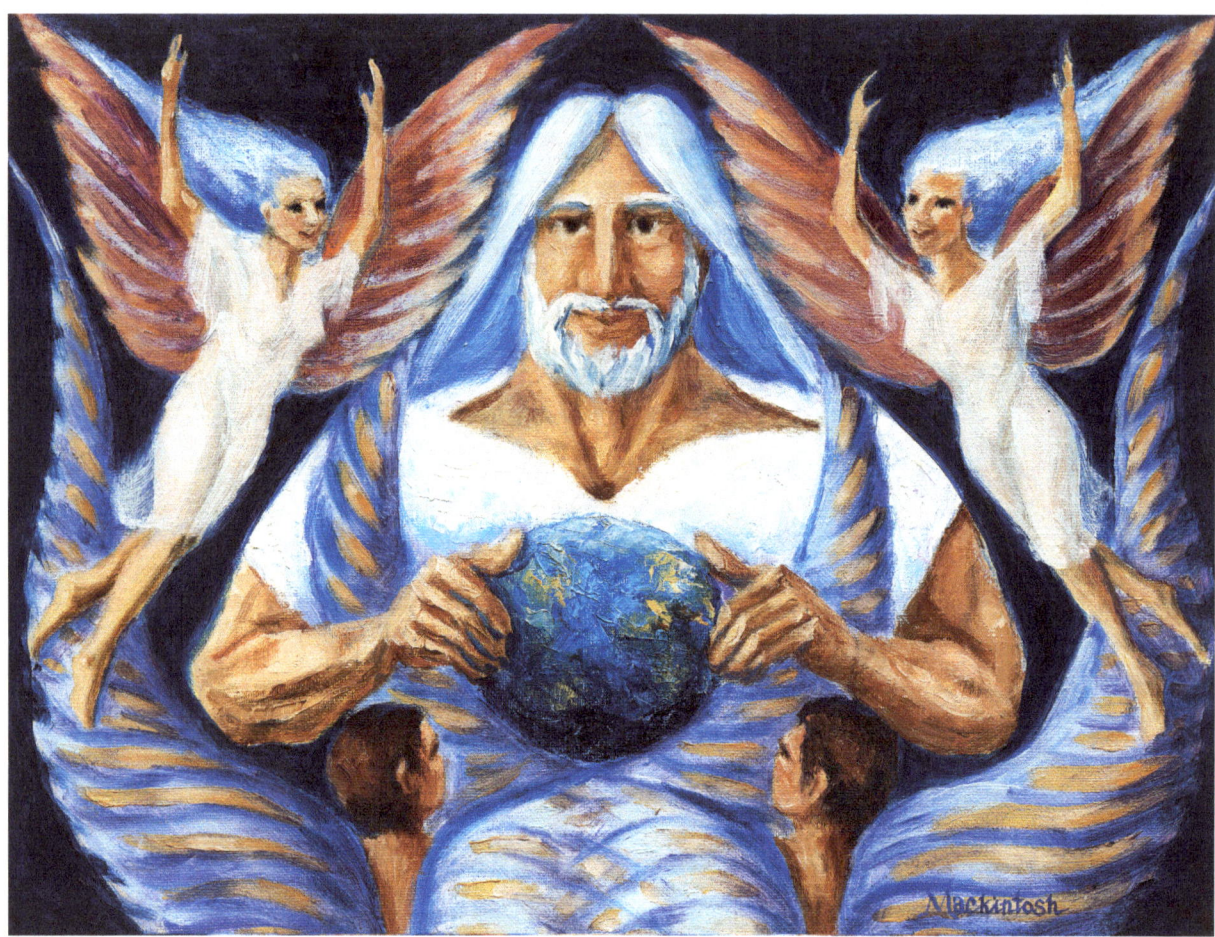

Painting 19: Omnipotence of the Redeemer

Nothing in the universe happens outside of our Creator's vision. His eyes follow to see that justice and righteousness prevail according to His will.

Meanwhile, as the above was happening, the Redeemer had compassion on his daughter Eve. He heard her cries as she poured her heart out to Him in spirit and in truth. He was touched by her sorrow and remembered His promise to her. That promise was not only for her comfort, but for ours also. He would fulfill His plan through her life bringing the promise of redemption for the whole world: He gave her another son, whose line would lead to the Redeemer.

God is way out in front of every event that happens or ever will happen. He knows every plan before it is planned and its outcome. Sometimes things go so badly and we suppose our Creator has abandoned us. But don't lose hope. Keep your faith. He is always faithful and will return to replace sorrow with joy. He is our Redeemer.

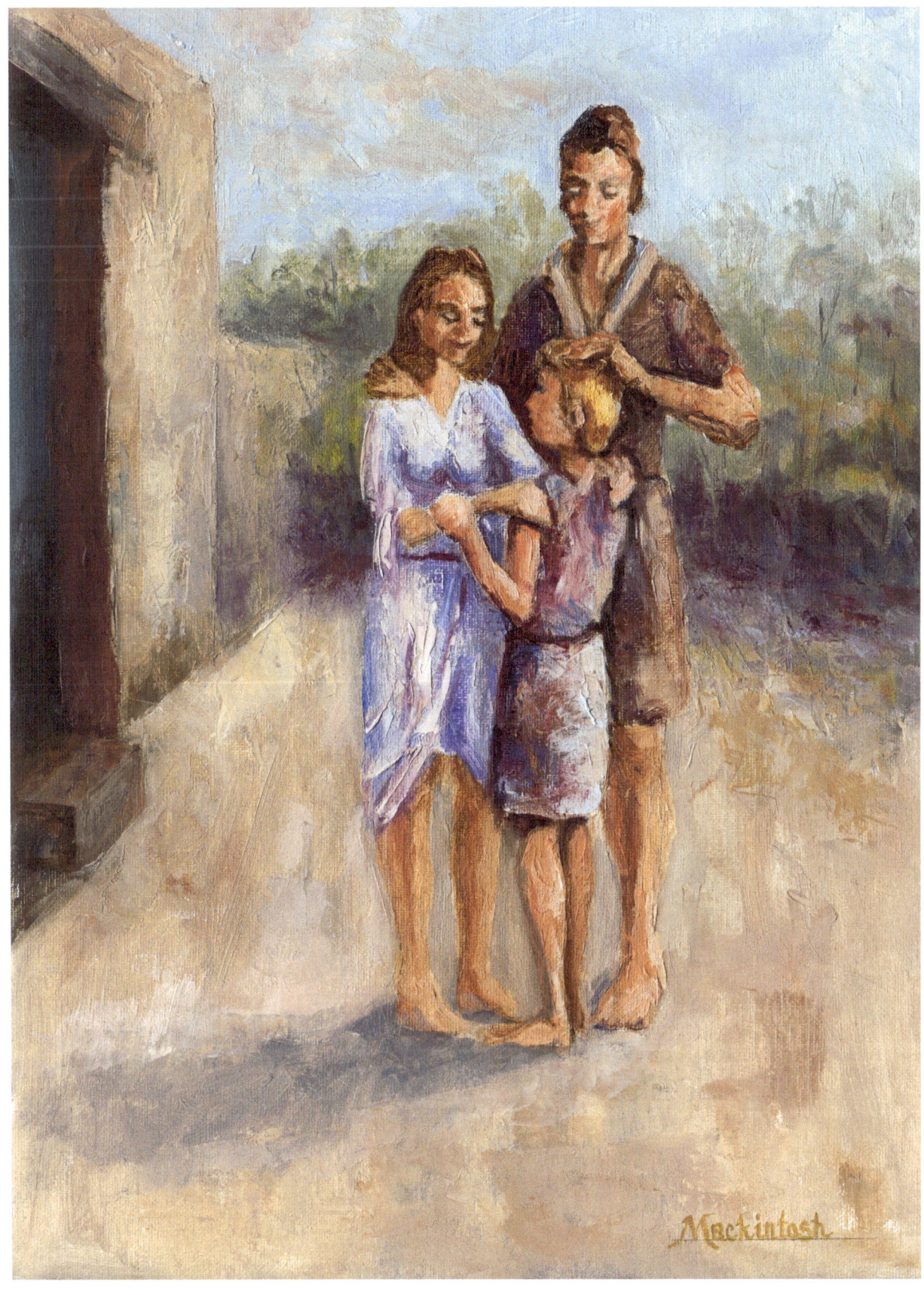

Painting 20: Seth, the Redeemer's Intervention

Seth, the Redeemers Intervention

(Gen 4:25) And Adam knew his wife again; and she bore a son, and called his name Seth: "For God," said she, "hath appointed me another seed instead of Abel, whom Cain slew."

God granted Adam and Eve another son to relieve the pain of Abel's death. They named him Seth. Adam and Eve purposed before God to raise him in the ways of the Lord, as they had Abel, to teach him the wisdom that God had taught them and never to depart from God's laws.

`As he grew, they saw that Seth was more than their comforter only. He, like Able, was special, having wisdom and grace to comfort others. He was humble before God, giving him thanks and glory every day from his heart.

Growing into manhood, Seth's wisdom became recognized by communities far and near. His judgments were true, just, and impartial. His counsel was compassionate, showing no respect to one's position or standing, but only what was just before God. He was esteemed for his prudence and sought for his counsel, a man of wisdom and virtue.

Adam and Eve saw God's hand of protection on Seth. They were content knowing that he would be the one to continue the chosen line of the Redeemer, which God had promised Eve: the seed of the woman that would crush the serpent's head. Seth's family eventually produced Noah, from whose line came our Redeemer.

The Prophecy of Enoch

(Jude 1:14) And Enoch also, the seventh from Adam, prophesied of these, saying, Behold, the Lord cometh with ten thousands of his saints, to execute judgment upon all, and to destroy all the ungodly and to convict all flesh of all the works of their ungodliness which they have ungodly committed, and of all the hard things which ungodly sinners have spoken against Him.

Six generations after Seth came Enoch, who was the great-grandfather of Noah. He gave the above prophecy, which was quoted in the New Testament by St. Jude. He lived sixty-five years and had a son, whom God instructed him to call Methuselah. (Fausset's Bible Dictionary signifies his name to mean: Methuselah, *"he dies and it shall be sent."*) God revealed to Enoch that Methuselah was to be a sign to the world that with the completion of his days, judgment would follow in the form of a flood. Enoch was struck with fear at God's hatred of the sin, corruption and violence that was covering the earth. He committed himself completely to God. He received visions and prophecies from God, which he communicated, warning the people. God showed him of the coming judgment of flood, and also revealed to him the coming of the Redeemer, which he also proclaimed to all. At this same time Adam also had a profound vision from God that a judgment of fire was also to come upon the earth.

The people saw that Enoch had great wisdom and the fear of the Lord guiding him so they appointed him to be their judge. Enoch taught them God's precepts of old, which had been lost from the time of Adam and his son Seth. The next three-hundred years Enoch preached repentance in preparation of the coming judgment. Much of the world returned again to follow the precepts of the Creator. Then one day God took him away.

The Bible states: *And Enoch walked with God; and was not; for God took him (Gen•5:24).* Also, *"By faith Enoch was translated that he should not see death; and was not found, because God had translated him: for before his translation he had this testimony, that he pleased God,"* (Hebrew 11:5).

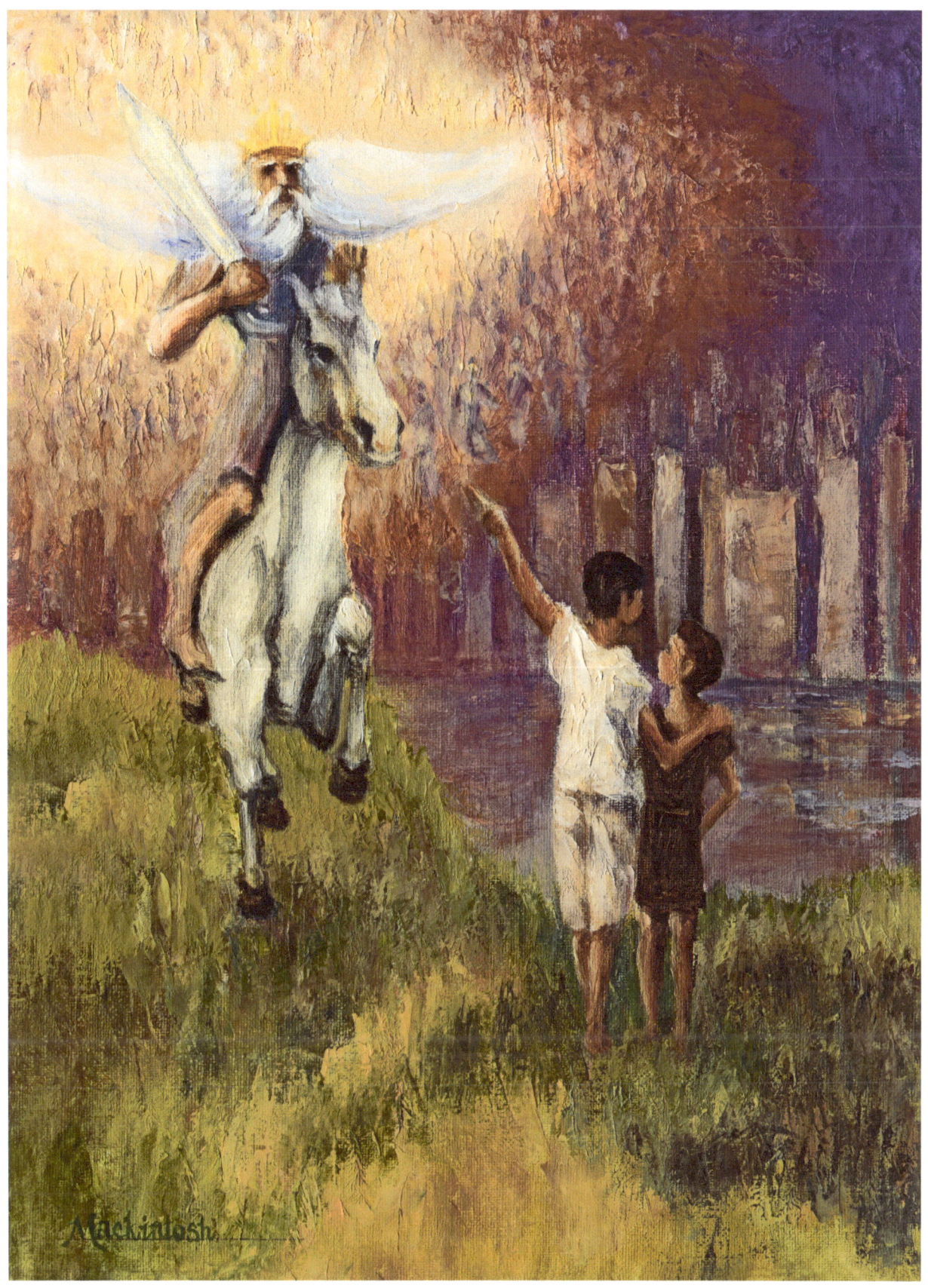

Painting 21: The Prophecy of Enoch

Amongst the antiquities discovered in the Qumran caves with the Dead-sea Scrolls, were fragments of the Book of Enoch. In this book was written the exact passage of text, word for word, recorded in the New Testament book of Saint Jude. Had the Creator preserved this book to reinforce his truth that states, *"My word will not pass away?"* Enoch was the first prophet ever to record the prophecy of Christ's return. He proclaimed, and wrote down this prophecy at least nine hundred years before the flood of Noah. It stands to this day. Not one word of our Redeemer will pass away.

The Sons of God and the Daughters of Men

(Gen 6:1-2, 4) When men began to multiply on the face of the earth, and daughters were born to them, the sons of God saw the daughters of men that they were fair; and they took them wives of all which they chose.... when the sons of God came in unto the daughters of men, and they bore children to them, the same became mighty men which were of old, men of renown.

As mankind continued to advance, multiply and grow in knowledge they became interested in new truths, more suited to their modern times. They disregarded the Creator's truth, and in time, even turned hostile to any knowledge of Him. New philosophies fired their thinking as they sought to fundamentally change ancient beliefs to make way for new truths. This led them away from God, their Creator and Redeemer. Ancient covenants and boundaries, which had been the standard, were now disdained, resulting in self-indulgence, lying, lust, greed, theft, hatred, indifference toward their neighbor, coveting, perversion, murder and disrespect for life. They rejected the Creator's laws, which opened the doors of their destruction.

The Jewish historian Josephus, in his writing, the *History of the Jewish People, 3:2*, commented that the posterity of Seth continued to esteem God as the Lord of the universe and to regard his virtues until the seventh generation. In the process of time, however, man grew further from God, forgot his laws and disregarding the ancient covenants that were handed down from Adam and Seth. They perverted God's truth, and abandoned practices of justice and instruction of their forefathers.

Commentaries by early church fathers suggested that, at this point in history, God assigned angels to the earth to instruct man how to beautify it. This by Justin Martyr: "God, when He had made the whole world, and subjected things earthly to man,...he committed the care of men and of all things under heaven to angels whom He appointed over them," (*Justin Martyr, chapter 5, Second Apology: How the Angels Transgressed*). Commodianus, in 240 A.D. commented also: "Almighty God, to beautify the nature of the world, willed that the earth should be visited by angels."

So when the angels of God (Sons of God) appeared, they were received as new gods who had the new truths they had been seeking. God had given these angels an assignment: to help man beautify and make advances on the earth. When these angels saw the beauty of earthly women, they were captivated and overcome with lust. Their craving was so great that they determined it would be worth giving up their eternal souls in exchange for these earthly women. So they made plans go against the Creator in order to quench the fire of their lust.

In fact, the prophet Enoch reports: They made a pact between themselves, "Come, let us choose us wives from among the children of men and beget us children....Let us all swear an oath, and all bind ourselves by mutual blasphemies not to abandon this plan but to do this thing." Then they swore all together and bound themselves by mutual curses upon themselves. There were two hundred in all who descended from heaven in the days of Jared on the summit of Mount Hermon, (Enoch 7:8. Although the *Book of Enoch* is considered as apocryphal, it was clearly known to early Christian writers, for example Jude 1:14; previously quoted).

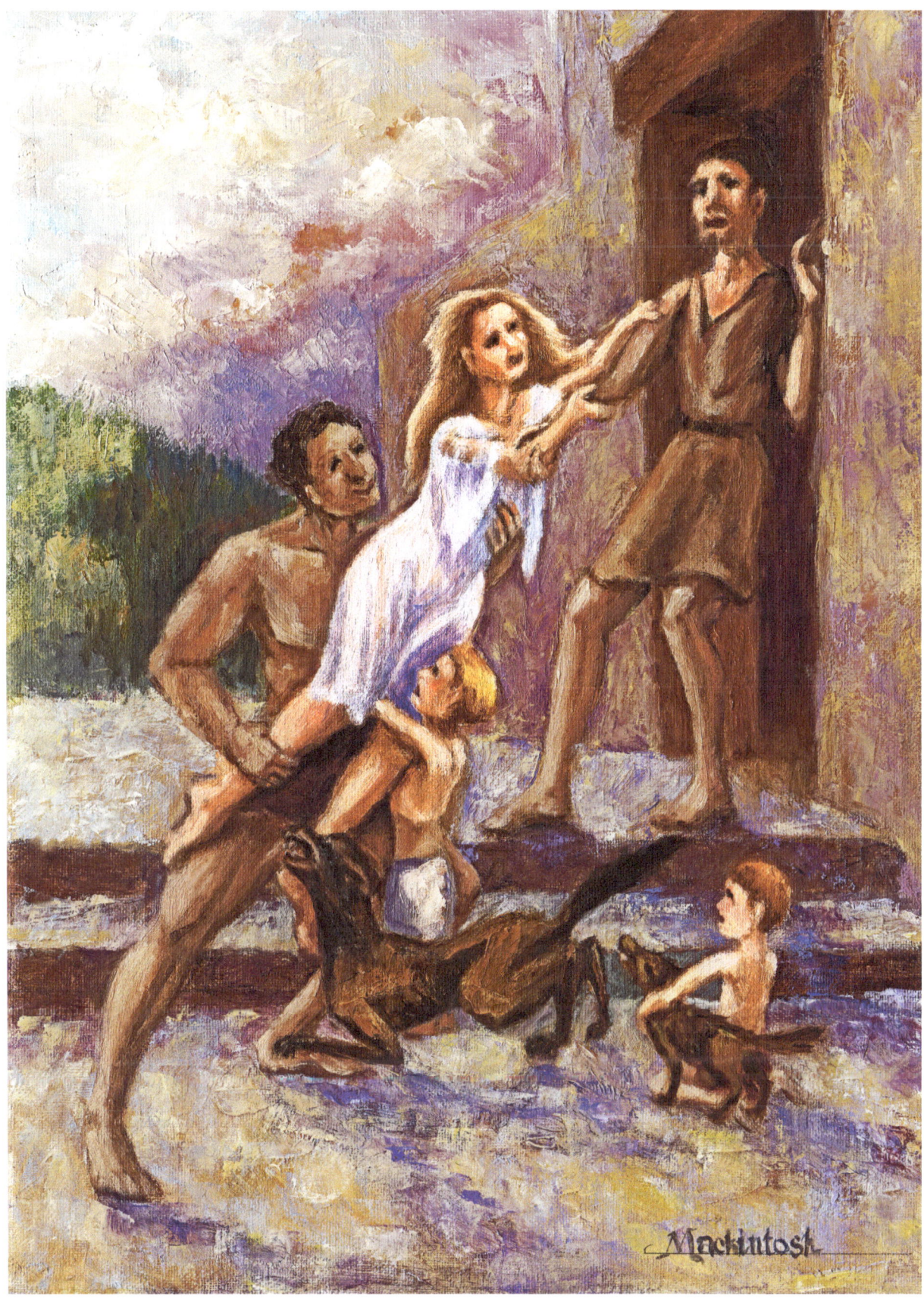

Painting 22: The Sons of God and the Daughters of Men

So the sons of God came in to the daughters of men [to whom] they bore children, called "nephilim." These were giants who lived on the earth in those days, and also afterward. They were the mighty men who were of old, men of renown (Gen 6:1).

Instead of helping man beautify the earth, these angels joined forces with Lucifer's fallen angels and went against God. Together they planned to pollute the seed of man with the seed of fallen angels and so, corrupt man's bloodline.

The book of Jasher states that these "rulers" (fallen angels) took wives for themselves by force, from their husbands. Also, the Sons of God took from the cattle of the earth, the beasts of the field and the fowls of the air, and began to mix and pollute different animals species, one with the other. This provoked the Lord; and God saw the whole earth and it was corrupt, for all flesh had corrupted its ways upon earth, all men and all animals (Jasher, Chapter 4:18; Apocryphal). Eventually the (giants) consumed all that man could produce until the people detested feeding them. So the giants turned against (the people) and began to eat them"(1 Enoch 7:1-5)

Their (giant) masters enslaved man using magic, fear and different punishments. They taught man how to appease them through enchantments, libations, sacrifices and to worship them as gods or worse would happen. *Whatever overcomes a person, to that he is enslaved.*

They also taught man acts of violence, and warfare, ways to harden metals for weapons: the making of sword, knives, axes, shields and breastplates so that they would kill one another and conquer. *Genesis 6:11 records that the earth was filled with violence. And the Lord said, "I will blot out man that I created from the face of the earth, yea from man to the birds of the air, together with cattle and beasts that are in the field."*

Ancient boundaries set by God were broken down and abandoned allowing evil to freely enter society. Their new deities taught them that life would be freer if they would fundamentally reject the precepts of old and do as they pleased. But it was a trap. Are we doing the same today? Seek wisdom and prudence now from our Redeemer.

Methuselah's Warning

(Gen 5:21-23,27) And Enoch lived sixty five years, and begat Methuselah. After he begat Methuselah, Enoch walked with God for three hundred years and begat sons and daughters. All the days of Methuselah were nine hundred sixty and nine years: and he died.

After the Lord took Enoch into heaven, the kings of the earth took Methuselah, his son, and anointed him to reign over them in place of his father. Methuselah lived uprightly in the sight of God all the days of his life, as his father Enoch had taught him. He carried on his father Enoch's ministry for the next six-hundred years, preaching the same warning from God as Enoch had. He taught the people wisdom, knowledge and the fear of God. All his days he did good turning neither to the right or the left.

During Methuselah's life, however, many people turned away from the Lord and corrupted the earth by plundering and robbing each other, rebelling against God, transgressing his ways and refusing to listen to the voice of Methuselah's warning. This brought on the Lord's anger and he stopped the seed they sowed from growing and brought up thorns and thistles instead. Still, mankind refused to repent and they continued doing evil against their Redeemer.

During these days Methuselah had a son named Lemech. When Lemech was one hundred and eighty years old he took Ashmua as his wife, who was the daughter of Elishaa, the son of Enoch, his uncle. They had a son whom Methuselah named Noah. Noah grew up and lived according to the ways of his father and Methuselah, perfect and upright with God.

As people multiplied on the face of the earth they all determined to do their own will, departing from the ways of the Lord. They also taught their sons and daughters their evil practices, continuing to sin against the Lord (condensed from *The Book of Jubilees chapter 4:vs 1-21;* translated by R. H. Charles, Society for Promoting Christian Knowledge, London, 1917).

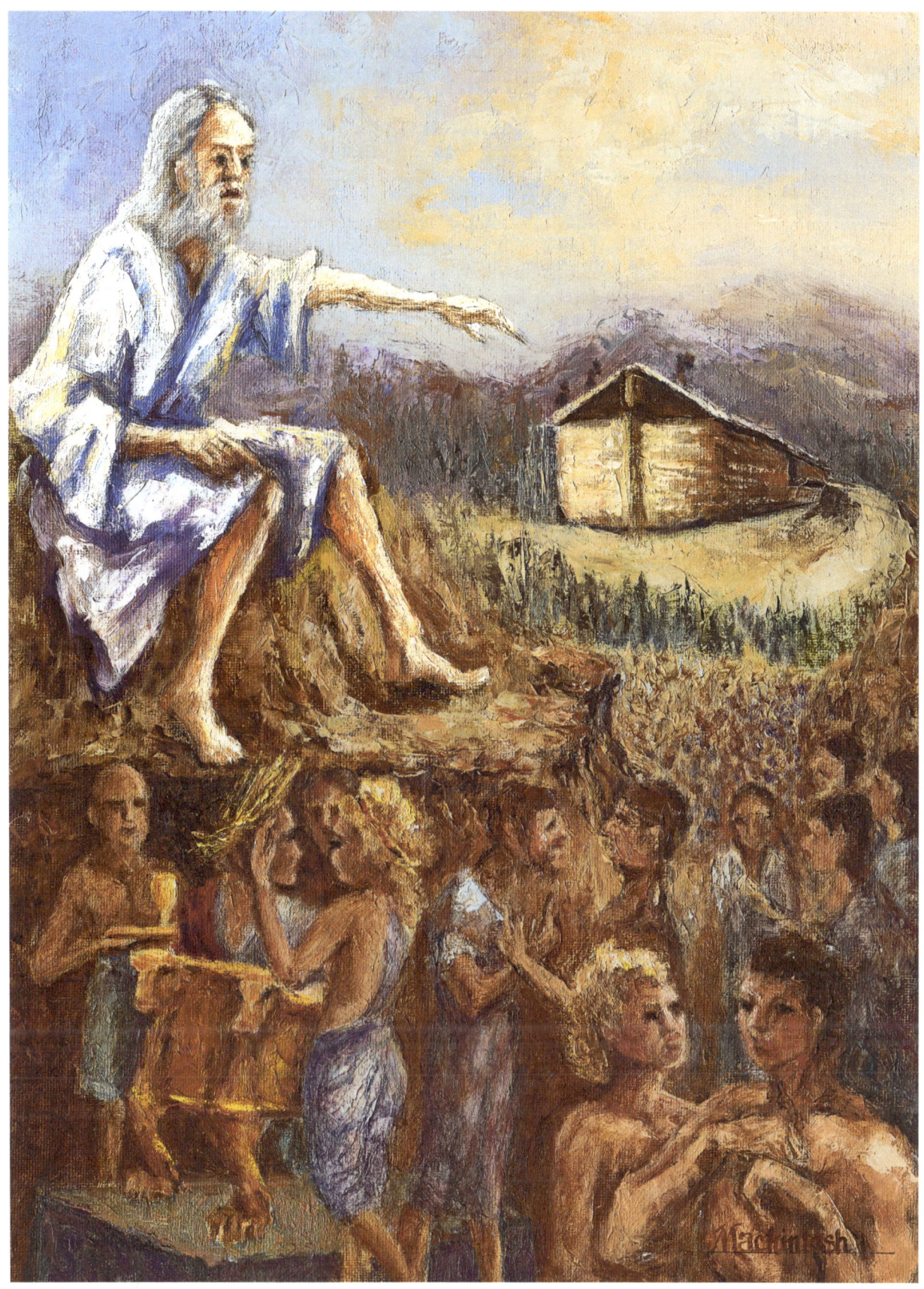

Painting 23: Methuselah's Warning

Meanwhile, Noah found favor in God's eyes who gave him plans to build an ark that would save human kind from the impending disaster: a flood that would cover the whole earth. So Noah and Methuselah continued to preach repentance: that all should return to their Redeemer before the destruction hit.

There are theologians who suggest that Methuselah died seven days before the start of Noah's flood. This gave Noah the traditional seven days to mourn and bury his grandfather. God had kept Methuselah alive to preach warning of the flood so that no one on earth would be taken by surprise and to return to their Redeemer. *God is not willing that any should parish but that all come to repentance (2 Peter 3:9):* But with Methuselah's death, time was up.

In this painting, the people of the world came out to watch Noah and Methuselah preach while partying with their friends. It was fun for them to jeer and mock that crazy preacher Methuselah and to heckle that fanatic Noah and his family. But Noah and Methuselah tirelessly kept warning of the Lord's coming judgment as the ark was being built.

The people of that day didn't believe a flood was possible. Nothing like that had ever happened. In fact, it was scientifically impossible. Unfortunately they all perished. They refused to listen to the warning of the Redeemer.

Salvation of the Redeemer

The Holy Bible states: *that if you will confess with your mouth that Jesus Christ is your Lord and believe in your heart that God has raised him from the dead you will be saved (Romans 10:9).*

In the days of old, our Redeemer instructed mankind that a sacrifice of blood, from a perfect lamb without any blemish, must be offered up to Him once every year to atone for their sins, making peace with God and to abate the curse of the ground. This rite was practiced for thousands of years by those whose hope was in God's redemption. Although God knew these sacrifices would never take away sins, it was still required until a better sacrifice could be offered.

Adam's sin brought death into the world. Offering the blood of a sacrificial lamb made atonement and spoke peace. When Cain killed Abel, Abel's blood cried out for vengeance, not peace. The sin of murder broke through the barrier that had restrained death. From then on the serpent's curse of death, hatred and murder flooded into the earth. Whenever ancient barriers are broken down the curses they had restrained will enter society like a flood. Since then, all of mankind has lived in darkness and the fear of death: that unknown country from whence no traveler returns. Death is the dreaded appointment we all must keep! Which also reveals to mankind our need of a better sacrifice than that of lambs.

So when the time was right, God provided Himself, for us, the perfect, sinless sacrifice that would satisfy His holy demands. He sent His only begotten Son Jesus, the Lamb of God, down from heaven to earth to die on the cross, to shed His blood, to take on Himself the death, suffering and punishment we deserve. By this He paid the debt of our sin for us. The sacrifice He provided does better than just covering our sins: it cleanses us from all our sin and gives us eternal life.

The blood of Abel cried out for vengeance: blood for blood against his murderer. But the blood of Christ Jesus, although we've sinned against God, speaks better things for us: redemption, eternal life and peace with God. After Jesus had suffered, died and was buried, since He was sinless, on the third day God raised Him up from death and He lives forevermore. He wants to raise you up to new life too. Trust Jesus Christ as your Redeemer, Savior and Lord of your life. He will give you new life.

The way to receive the Redeemer's redemption is to admit to him that you are a sinner, tell him that you want to turn away from your sins and accept the sacrifice He made for you on the cross by shedding his own blood to wash away your sins. If you truly believe this with your whole heart and speak this with your mouth, you will be saved.

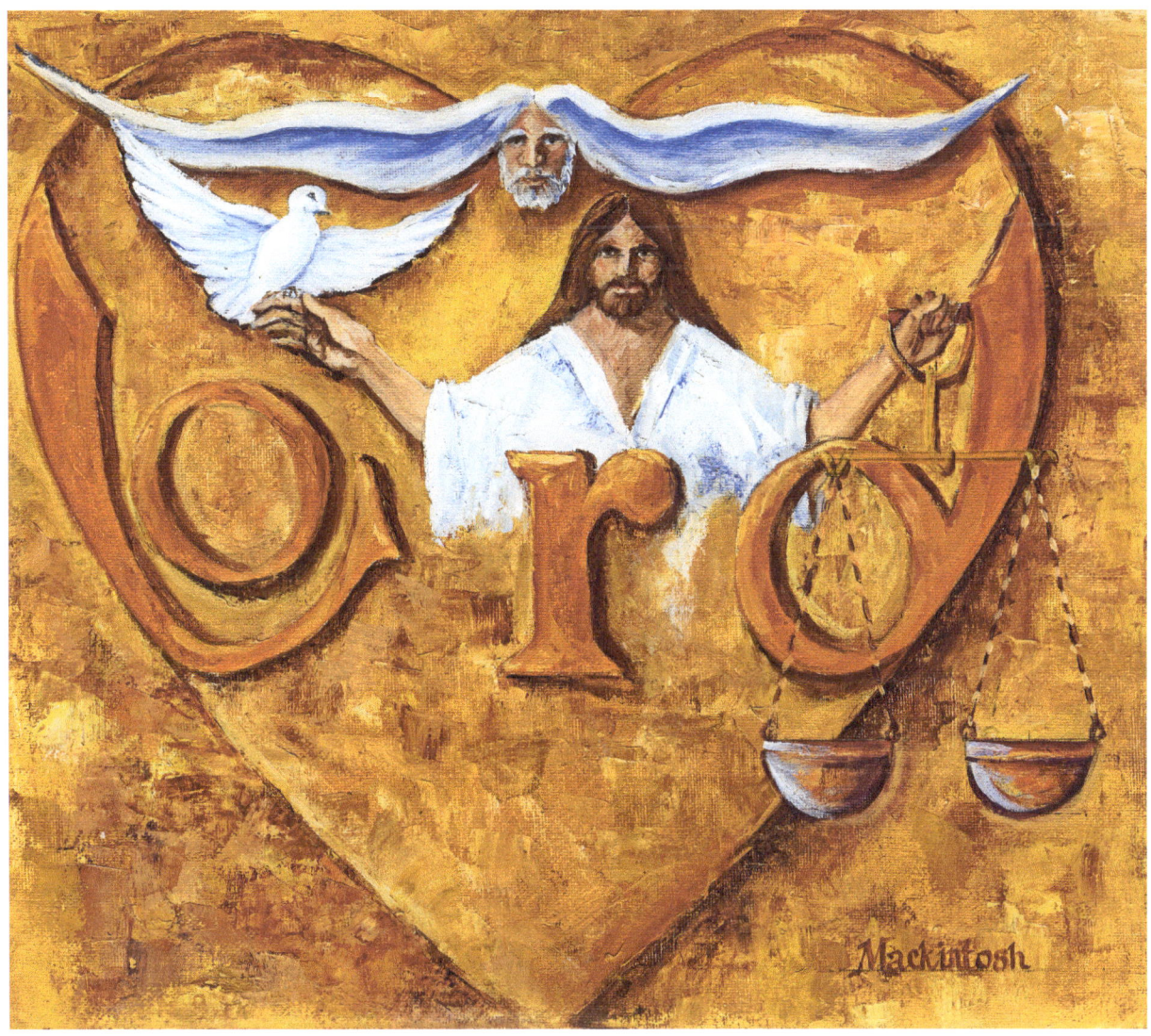

Painting 24: Salvation of the Redeemer

Here is a short prayer:

Lord Jesus, I believe you are my Redeemer, but I am a sinner. I've sinned against you greatly. I want to turn away from my sin. I believe that you died on the cross and shed your blood to cleanse me of my sin. I believe that God raised you from death on the third day to give me new life. Cleanse me, save me and give me new life, Lord. I trust you now to be my Redeemer and Lord. Change me from the darkness of death to the light of life. I confess that you, Jesus, are my Lord, my Redeemer and my Savior. Amen.

Tell someone close to you about your decision. Get a Bible and read it. It's His word. As you read it, ask the Holy Spirit to guide you to find God's special path for your life and to understand His will for you. He is your Redeemer.

www.ingramcontent.com/pod-product-compliance
Lightning Source LLC
Chambersburg PA
CBHW040751200526
45159CB00025B/1847